Praise for Robert Steele and *Steele Here*

"*Steele Here* will make you feel like you are in the Cowboys training camp sweating every cut and wanting to make the team. I loved this book."

—**Roger Staubach**
Heisman Trophy winner,
Dallas Cowboys Super Bowl Champion quarterback and MVP

"Having seen Robert in action on and off the field, the principles he applies to his work every day are valuable guides for anyone striving to achieve. His book inspires us to make our dreams a reality."

—**Richard Anderson**
CEO, Delta Airlines

"In my mind, Robert is *Steele Here* working hard, planning smartly, and making things happen. This is a book that everyone in the family can enjoy."

—**Gene Stallings**
Former head football coach of Texas A&M, Saint Louis/Phoenix Cardinals, and the
University of Alabama National Champions of 1992

"I saw Robert, in action, putting these principles to work even before I knew the *Steele Here* story. Robert lives this every day. You should, too."

—**Bob Greczyn**
Former CEO, BCBS NC

"Having been a free agent myself, I really enjoyed reading *Steele Here*. Having been a coach while he was going through his trials of trying to become a Dallas Cowboy made it more special. This is a book everyone will enjoy."

—**Dan Reeves**
Head coach of the Denver Broncos and Atlanta Falcons, a player for the Dallas
Cowboys in two Super Bowls, and a coach in four Super Bowls

"Everybody in business and life needs a kick in the pants when the obstacles seem too big, the mountain too high to climb. *Steele Here* reminded me of what separates the doers in life from the talkers and posers—grit and unwillingness to accept failure as an option. Read Robert's story and you will forget the excuses and get to next level . . . wherever or whatever the next level is in your life."

—Tobin Smith
Fox News

"This is a story of great passion and deep determination, an inspiration as well as a path for all of us who hope to achieve. Robert Steele played football at the highest level, but more importantly, he has lived life in the same way."

—Dr. William Cale
President, University of North Alabama

"Robert has brought the sports outcomes into his business world by making things happen full speed every day. You too will dream much bigger as a result of reading this book."

—Butch Johnson
Former Dallas Cowboys receiver

"*Steele Here* is part motivation, part inspiration, part perspiration, and part execution. All of these ingredients are what you need to dream bigger dreams."

—Gil Brandt
Former vice president of player personnel, Dallas Cowboys
Current Sirius NFL Radio Network Host

STEELE
HERE

STEELE HERE

An Underdog's Secret to Success

Robert Steele
Former Dallas Cowboy, Super Bowl XIII

Brown Books Publishing Group
Dallas, Texas

Steele Here
An Underdog's Secret to Success

Brown Books Publishing Group
16250 Knoll Trail Drive, Suite 205
Dallas, Texas 75248
www.brownbooks.com
(972) 381-0009

A New Era in Publishing.™

ISBN 978-1-61254-010-8
Library of Congress Control Number 2011928386

Printed in the United States.
10 9 8 7 6 5 4 3 2 1

For more information about Robert or the book,
please visit www.SteeleHere.com.

Steele Here is dedicated to my parents, Richard and Carol Steele. Our family lost both of them to different illnesses in 2002. I'm not sure how many families have experienced the loss of both parents in the same year through an illness. However, we were able to celebrate their fiftieth wedding anniversary on February 2, 2002, just prior to our father's death in March and our mother's in August.

They were wonderful parents who taught me character, compassion, conviction, and allowed my creativity to become a part of my developing sense of self as I grew up. I have so many fond memories of growing up, and while we had good times and bad—as all families experience—the good is all I truly remember (though that may be part of the selective memory we all enjoy as years pass by).

Mother and Dad, we still miss you every day. I am often engaged in conversations where I hear folks say, "I have to go see my parents." I think silently, I wish I had that ability. You both would have appreciated the book and enjoyed sharing the stories that you lived or heard as I experienced the ups and downs of being the least probable Cowboy in 1978. I miss you more than I am able to communicate through the written word.

Contents

Foreword

People ask me what Coach Tom Landry's secret was—how and why he was able to create the football dynasty he did with the Dallas Cowboys. I tell them what Landry told us all: "Football is a game of inches and of balls bouncing for the good or bad. But isn't it interesting that the better-prepared team always seems to have the ball bounce their way?"

Simple as it is, that is the Coach Landry preparation mantra. Any player who didn't make that mantra their own didn't do very well on the field or after they left football. Preparation is the key to success, and nobody knew that better than Tom Landry. Coach Landry knew where he was going, how he was going to get there, and what bus he was taking to arrive on time. If you weren't on that bus, you weren't going with him.

A lot of men have played ball for Coach Landry, and I've coached or played with more of them than I can remember. Robert Steele was one of them. He played one season with the Cowboys as one of my receivers and special-team players, and I vividly recall how he played. The best thing I remember about him is that he practiced as hard as he played. When he writes about going full speed every day on every play, he really did. In practice and in the games, you could count on him being near the action every play. Robert would catch any ball thrown his way, run as many routes for our quarterbacks as their arms would throw, and sacrifice his body on special teams. He had such an upbeat, positive attitude you could not help but want to see what was going to happen.

In 1978, as today, every player who made the forty-five-man Dallas Cowboys roster had to be among the very best. When Robert first arrived, we were not sure how he might turn out. But he kept at it. He kept making plays that got coaches' attention. Free agents have to do that. In the end, he accomplished his goal. I believe Robert was able to capture the essence of the Dallas Cowboys mentally as well as physically and was determined to be a success. Success was important. But win or lose, improving every time you played was even more important. This is what coaches look for in new players.

When I mention the essence of the Dallas Cowboys organization, I mean to say that it was more than just a football team. The Dallas Cowboys were a first-class organization from the top all the way down to the bottom. Our owner, Clint Murchison, created the division of labor; Tex Schramm created the "America's Team" vision and managed all aspects of the front office; and Tom Landry was allowed to coach the team to always put the best product on the field to represent the organization.

Schramm and Landry were two very different personalities who were each allowed—even encouraged—to excel in their respective duties. Very few organizations prior to or even since then have gelled to the point where the Cowboys were in the mid-seventies. Robert joined the team during our golden years, at the pinnacle of success after our win against the Denver Broncos in Super Bowl XII.

Robert arrived on the scene with little more than a wing and a prayer of replacing our four returning veteran wide receivers. Drew Pearson was one of the best ever to play the game. Tony Hill, Butch Johnson, and the other starter opposite Drew in Super Bowl XII, Golden Richards, would have caused any draft choice, let alone a free agent, to doubt their chances of success. It was the best of times for the Cowboys and the worst of times for players hoping to replace some of the best talent in professional football.

Steele, like many players, had the unique advantage not only of seeing Coach Landry's pioneering coaching approach really bear fruit, but of playing with some incredible football legends. He did more than just play, watch, and observe. Over the years he's taken time to put the lessons from Tom Landry down for others to read and appreciate, and now he has collected those lessons in his first book, *Steele Here*.

Robert's book is about success. It is also about preparation. It is about setting goals. All of these concepts are not "new news" to you and me. However, Robert has a way of weaving the stories together to bring them to life and make you feel like you are almost there in Thousand Oaks, California, as he is trying to dream his impossible dream.

As I said, this book is about success. It truly is. But it's not just about a season of success. It's about a lifetime of successes built on one tremendous effort, the lessons he learned from having been a part of the Cowboys legacy, and the pride of playing for Coach Tom Landry.

I had the unique advantage of playing for, coaching for, and coaching against the Cowboys, and I always respected Coach Landry for the discipline, character, and quality of team he put on the field. The Cowboys were pioneers in their approach to scouting players, their use of computers in analyzing games and game situations at every angle, and the invention of the Flex defense, all of which gave the Cowboys an advantage at every turn.

I have been involved in football my entire life. You could say I was born to play, and I will die watching the game. It is in my blood. Growing up in the steel town of Aliquippa, Pennsylvania, I quickly realized that sports was going to be my ticket ahead.

Playing college football and being drafted to play in the NFL was my dream come true. It meant that I could keep playing a kid's game for as long as I was physically able. Of course, the "physically able" part has caught up to me, having had knee replacement on both knees (twice) and hip replacements on both hips (also twice). This is the price that all players pay to play this game. This is one reason that I am passionate about helping former players with my Gridiron Greats program.

The goal of every season is to win the Super Bowl. I was fortunate to be a part of more than a few Super Bowl games with some great teams and great guys. Winning the Super Bowl three times, one as a player, one as an assistant coach, and one as the head coach of the Chicago Bears, coaching one of the best teams ever in 1985, was a special time and provides great memories for me. Taking home the Vince Lombardi trophy is something you will always remember. Yet in the world of professional football no team is ever allowed to rest on its laurels for more than a few weeks. The next season comes too quickly, and every other team will be knocking on your door to knock you off your pedestal of success.

When I speak to audiences today, it is always about more than just football. It is about life lessons learned by watching others. People enjoy the stories about certain games, interesting facts about certain players, and how I reacted during certain situations. I enjoy sharing those things, but what I enjoy the most is sharing from the heart about character. Being a winner inside is always about being true to yourself and leaving the audience with an understanding that setting goals, accomplishing those goals, and darn sure setting *more* goals is how you will achieve greatness on the football field or the field of life.

Coach Landry was the authority figure in our lives, almost "godlike." This was because we feared him, respected him, and more importantly, wanted to please him. You felt like a million dollars when he complimented you on a particular play for a great block or catch. You felt like a tin can when he would run a bonehead play over and over without saying a word. He commanded the respect of his players, his coaches, and everyone associated with the Cowboys—and, for that matter, everyone he encountered. That is why we became America's team. People expected us to win. We drafted great players and we top-graded our talent every year. We pushed our players to know every play, in every situation, and what defense they might see based on particular formations. No detail was left to chance.

Of course, it is still a game. Yes, a game of inches. A game of breaks. A game that does resemble organized chaos many times. But it is also a well-orchestrated, almost choreographed, display of fluid motion. In the end, it comes down to preparation. Proper preparation always prevents poor performance. Well, almost always. While every game plan is prepared to win every game, sometimes you come up short. The next week you go back and prepare harder for the next game. Like the old saying goes, success is never final and failure is never fatal. Keep trying, keep learning, and keep your head up.

You will enjoy this book for three reasons: One, it is about football and life. Two, it is about an era in our world on which we are able to look back and remember a simpler time where honesty and integrity were secured with a handshake, not a contract. Finally, it is about understanding how individual effort and attitude consistently delivered by unique individuals allows a team to accomplish extraordinary results. I believe that, and I believe you will not only enjoy reading *Steele Here*, you will see yourself differently after closing the book.

—Mike Ditka
December 2010

Acknowledgments

I initially wrote *Steele Here* to allow Remington, Abigail, Savannah, and Travis to understand why their father is "wired" the way he is. My quirky little sayings, my positive attitude, my always wanting the best for each of them, and my undying love for each of them are the reasons for this book. I wanted them to know the story of my life, before they were born, that drove me to want the best for each of them. I get up every morning—too early, many times!—to show them the way. While I am not a perfect person, my love for them is perfected through time.

This book could not have been possible without hundreds—possibly thousands—of people. So it is not possible to name them all. If you helped or supported me in my life up until this point, and I do not name you personally, you are to be thanked, and I will thank you in person at the appropriate time.

I only wish my mother and father could be here to see that I was able to put more than four sentences together in a paragraph and more than four paragraphs into a book. They were proud of all of my accomplishments, few as they were, and allowed me to dream all of my *big* dreams every day of my life. I miss them every day.

My dear sister Vicki has always been my biggest supporter and fan. She has been in my corner when no one else was. If I ever give you another company, turn it down. My sister Susan was always a better athlete than I was, and if Title IX had only come around a few years earlier, she would have been a three-sport star.

My brother Ricky got my Super Bowl check, as my first investment, which taught me a lot about investing.

I want to thank Caron Goode for taking my random writings, all written while flying coast to coast on Delta Airlines, and turning that into something we could actually call a book. Wynton Hall turned the preliminary writings into a book with words that actually "pop" off the page. For that, I am grateful. Wynton, you rock.

The Dallas Cowboys took a chance on a free agent whom no one else would have. The Cowboys will always be my first love.

There are so many people who influenced my life before 1978 and for many years after. It would take way too many paragraphs to name you all. You are the fabric of my life. My years growing up in Columbus, Georgia, college days at UNA, the people in Dallas and Minneapolis during my short NFL career, and the people who helped shape my life as a salesperson will always be near and dear to me. Some have passed on, and I wish I could thank them one final time. For those who have passed on and those whose paths I have crossed, I truly appreciate what you have done to make my life special. For that, I am eternally grateful.

Finally, I would be remiss not to say thanks to all of the coaches who spent countless hours helping me when I could not walk and chew gum at the same time. Yes, I was awkward throughout most of my early athletic life. I had some great moments and plenty of times when I wondered what I was even doing on a field. But there were coaches who supported me, coached me, and even loved me when I was struggling to play at each level.

Prologue
Pregame Warm-Up

You know what I miss most about playing professional football?

I miss the hitting. Hard, purposeful, pad-to-pad and helmet-to-helmet contact against a man who wanted to beat me to the ball—and beat me up—as much as I wanted to make him look bad in front of his hometown fans.

I miss the lessons I learned every day from legendary Dallas Cowboys coach Tom Landry. I can see him now, stalking the sidelines, arms folded across his chest, fedora firmly in place, controlling a game like no other coach before or since.

I miss the challenge of striving to make every play a work of art, my routes Van Goghs and Rembrandts that would confuse defensive backs and give our offense a chance to put points on the board.

I miss the smell of fresh-mown grass on the practice field, the sun peeking over the horizon, the air thick with humidity and the promise of another day of practice as coaches' shouts and whistles called us to action.

I miss talking with the players on my team—fast friends with a common goal—in the locker room after a hard practice, sweating and laughing and crying and hurting together with the effort that we hoped would take us to the Super Bowl.

Odd as it seems, I even miss the aches and the pains. They reminded me that I was still alive—and mortal.

You know what I miss most about playing professional football?

Hell, just about everything.

For two seasons, one with the Dallas Cowboys and one with the Minnesota Vikings, I had the rare opportunity to do what every boy growing up in the 1960s dreamed of—and so few experienced.

The Super Bowl era in the NFL began in the late 1960s, but it was a decade or so before that the league began its unprecedented rise in sports as the country's most popular pastime. My idols were guys like Ray Nitschke, the Green Bay Packers' linebacker most people remember for his ferocious tackling, his intimidating sneer, and a bloody, ripped uniform draped on him with the fearful elegance of a gladiator's armor. Every exposed surface was covered with athletic tape; mud hung from the facemask of his helmet—and none of it stopped him from wreaking havoc on opponents.

And then there was Lance "Bambi" Alworth, the San Diego Chargers and Dallas Cowboys wide receiver who brought a new standard of athleticism to the game and opened the door for wide receivers to play in more explosive offenses. He leapt for passes with a dancer's grace, cut routes like a cheetah on the prowl.

Every evening, my friends and I would play football in the yard until the last shred of light had been wrung out of the day, imitating our favorite players and wondering what it would be like to experience just one snap in the NFL.

The next evening, we would do it again.

I had passion for the game—who didn't?—and maybe enough talent to get by. Pretty quickly, I figured out that nothing was going to get me to the top faster than hard work and dedication to a goal. But I also had mentors and coaches who not only told me that I could succeed, they showed me how.

And that's what I want to do in *Steele Here*, which chronicles my journey as an underdog from a small Southern campus at the University of North Alabama to the training camp of the Dallas Cowboys—America's Team—to the Super Bowl, the most-watched sporting event on the planet.

Too many young people give up their dreams because of a lack of opportunity. The more you let go of your dreams, the easier it becomes to forget that you even have them.

I've learned quite a few lessons along the way, but none of them more important than this: The key to achieving the big dream isn't just setting a goal. You've also got to take action to accomplish that goal, charting new courses—and always dreaming bigger dreams.

I overcame my share of obstacles—as an undrafted free agent in the NFL, the chances of making an opening-day roster are pretty slim—and had my eyes opened to a world where football doesn't resemble sport so much as barely organized chaos, a violent ballet where the idea is to pummel your opponent into submission while scoring more points.

Ever felt like an underdog?

Join the club!

I can identify with you and give you practical, workable ideas about how to achieve your own success.

Just like me, you relate to the fact that underdogs train harder and longer to make every break count and to overcome odds no bookie in his right mind would ever take (one newspaper called the odds of my making the Cowboys after signing a free-agent contract a million-to-one).

All I ever wanted was one more shot, one more day of practice. And in the end, I turned that impossible dream into reality. In *Steele Here*, I come back to some common themes, using my own experiences as a guide.

What was life like for a long shot trying to make the team? That question applies to your life whether you're passionate about playing professional football, managing a small business, raising a family, or accomplishing an extraordinary goal you've set for yourself.

What lessons do underdogs learn that others don't, and how can we best apply those in our daily lives? The underdog knows how tough it is to be recognized, earn respect, and become more than an afterthought.

Throughout *Steele Here*, I share my secrets to success in sections called "Red Zone Rules," named for the place on the football field that every offense wants to get into so they can score.

And I've created an acronym—TEAM: Together our Effort and Attitude create Momentum—as a model for helping you to achieve your ultimate dream. Effort and attitude separate the underdog from the pack. Underdogs elevate themselves through effort and attitude. What you'll come to find is that achieving your dreams is just a matter of asking yourself two questions: "Am I dreaming *big enough*?" and "Will I do whatever it takes to accomplish my goals?"

I took the concept of TEAM from my time with the Dallas Cowboys, a team whose work ethic, attitude, talent—and even swagger—characterized American sports and set the standard by which NFL franchises are measured even today. I'm looking forward to sharing my TEAM philosophy with stories of student-athletes, coaches, corporations, C-suite executives, and players from all walks of life.

What's the most important predictor of success?

Give me someone with a great attitude who will give their best effort, and more often than not, they'll beat your best athlete.

Effort and *attitude* separate the mediocre from the best. At almost any skill level, when abilities and talents are similar, the greatest differentiators are the two aspects of outcome that we control and will win us games and championships when adversity comes our way.

Every coach in America loves the one player who will give a great effort with a great attitude even without possessing great talent. Talent is necessary, of course, but there are many talented people not achieving their dreams because their attitude and effort are lacking. Even today, football is full of players who have all the talent in the world, but have a tough time taking constructive criticism. For those guys, NFL means "Not for Long."

I remember the day I became a Dallas Cowboy as clearly as any event in my life, almost as if I had stepped over an imaginary line—the line we often set for ourselves that usually acts as a self-fulfilling prophecy—and started living my dream.

Making the forty-five-man roster for America's Team was an "overnight success" story more than fifteen years in the making, a story of intense preparation, months of sacrifice, dedication, and commitment to the goal—and, always, the will to never give in. I'm hoping that my story of America's Team will change the way you view yourself, the goals you set, and what you expect from your life.

Steele Here is the story of my journey to the NFL and beyond—and the journey to the success that you've always imagined.

1

Underdog

The Return of America's Team (Spring 1978)

On January 15, 1978, the Dallas Cowboys celebrated their return to the top of the NFL in Super Bowl XII in New Orleans by dismantling the Denver Broncos and their popular "Orange Crush" defense, winning by a final score of 27–10.

Dallas was led by superstar quarterback Roger Staubach and a Hall of Fame cast of characters—including their phenomenal running back, Heisman Trophy winner Tony Dorsett, out of the University of Pittsburgh, who would keep the Cowboys competitive for another decade. And Randy White, Harvey Martin, and the rest of the Cowboys' "Doomsday Defense" put the exclamation point on one of the most lopsided Super Bowls to date.

The victory left no doubt the Cowboys were back. And that scared a lot of teams.

Despite finishing 11–3 the previous season, the Cowboys limped to an early-round play-off exit the year before. Like every worthy champion, though, the team rebounded.

Sure, slick marketing reinforced America's belief that the Cowboys were *their* team. After all, they had a guy dressed in a gaudy cowboy outfit leading cheers during games.

Oh, and they had the cheerleaders.

But hard work, a dedicated collection of players, and outstanding coaches won America's hearts as much as any of the glitz and glimmer.

The math's pretty simple: Win and you're beloved. Lose, though, and your fans wear paper sacks on their heads when they come to the stadium (remember the 'Aints, who finally have an S on the front of their jerseys after decades of disappointments and a resounding victory in Super Bowl XLIV).

When it came to the NFL, fans expected America's Team to win every year.

In the week following Super Bowl XII, twenty-seven other teams focused on knocking the Cowboys from their pedestal.

Win a division or a play-off game, and you're a good team.

Win a Super Bowl, and you're in the bullseye for every other team in the league. There are no easy games in the NFL. Gil Brandt, the Cowboys general manager and draft guru, would lead the draft selections in 1978, paving the way for draft choices, free agents, and veterans to embark on the team's quest to retain the legendary Vince Lombardi trophy—and to gain football immortality.

Underdog

I wasn't the best player on my University of North Alabama football team.

I wasn't even the best player on my Hardaway High School team in Columbus, Georgia.

In fact, I played fewer than ten snaps during my freshman year of high school as a scout team "dummy" (not a term that inspires a lot of confidence in a young man). The experience upset me enough to quit football the next year, but loneliness—and the addictive camaraderie of the gridiron—compelled me to return to the team. I changed positions, determined not to warm the bench.

And my strategy wasn't successful.

I sat on the bench my junior year of high school as well, making an appearance as a holder for extra points but never seeing action as a third-string quarterback.

Our head coach left to go across town to a small private high school, and another coach was brought in. The assistants knew of my desire to play and, sensing my frustration, moved me to tight end for my senior season. I had good hands, I could block a little, and I came off the ball well. But I had never seen any game action. I earned the starting spot at tight end, caught twenty-five passes, kicked off, and kicked all the extra points. The coaches awarded me the Most Improved Player trophy for the amazing turn-around from a season before.

Going from perennial bench warmer to starter and being voted All Bi-City by the Columbus newspapers was an improvement, but those numbers hardly warranted a college scholarship, something I had not factored in to the equation.

Still, the University of North Alabama, a small college northwest of Columbus in Florence, Alabama, invited three Hardaway players for a campus visit. They wanted our superstars, of course, my teammates and friends Mike McGlamry, the quarterback, and Jessie Murray, a wide receiver. But because I was close to those guys, I was in the mix. Coach Fred Marceaux, who later became one of the top lieutenants in the A. L. William's multilevel marketing company and made millions selling insurance, drove the three of us to UNA for a campus visit in my dad's car. The UNA coaches thought that the only way to get Mike and Jessie would be to offer all three of us scholarships.

They offered.

Even though football should have ended for me when I left the field on Senior Night in high school, UNA offered me a chance to continue to play football (college recruiting was quite a bit different in the 1970s!).

I accepted.

Football wasn't my passion, at that time. Baseball was. But I figured I could pay for my college education by playing football and maybe be able to play baseball as well.

It's no exaggeration to say that I arrived at the University of North Alabama unprepared for college. Arriving with no study skills, I also arrived with a body not even close to ready for college football, even at the Division II level. I had never lifted weights, never exerted more energy than was absolutely necessary to play ball—any ball, at any level—and though I had the ability to keep me playing long enough to move to the next level (at least as far as college), I realized I was an underdog as soon as I stepped foot on campus.

Understand: I was an underdog because I had put myself in that position.

The real world was about to wake me up to what price I would pay to play at the next level. In the spring of 1975, my freshman year, my left knee was blown out by a linebacker who speared me after an interception. Nine months later, I had a second surgery—this one on my right knee—that showed me I was in no shape to play college football.

In hindsight, those injuries worked in my favor. The excruciating pain of the surgery, the months on crutches, and the yearning brought on by watching others excel while I was once again stuck on the sideline—all those things taught me some valuable lessons that I soon began to apply to my daily life.

I worked hard enough to become a starter in my junior year at UNA, making second-team All-Conference and leading the conference with thirty receptions on a team better known for its running game. Senior season saw a change in the coaching staff and even more running plays. I caught only twenty-five balls that season—after grabbing fifteen in my first three games—but I led the Gulf South Conference in receiving yardage and was voted first-team All-Conference.

Suddenly, though, my football-playing days were over.

It was a nice way to end my career at UNA, and I figured years later, when I looked back on those days, I would have a few good memories and maybe a story or two for my children and grandchildren.

Cue Bruce Springsteen's "Glory Days," right?

In spring 1978, I moved out of the athletic dorm and spent my last semester in Florence with a fraternity brother, Mark Spry. I decided to become more involved in the campus life of UNA, participating in FIJI fraternity activities and increasing my dating. UNA had plenty of available talent since three previous Miss Alabamas were attending UNA. They were all Phi Mus, and I had my eye on a Phi Mu myself.

Three or four of the jocks from UNA thought they were good enough to play pro football, and they were headed to a scouting combine camp for tryouts in Atlanta. They asked me to go with them—not because they thought I should try out, but because I was the one with the car. College football players did not generally have money for road trips. The guys never knew why I always was able to do things. They were not aware that I was receiving more than one hundred dollars a month in commissions from my summer job two years before and I saved all of my summer job money prior to my senior year. I was saving it for a nice long vacation prior to starting back in the insurance business after graduation. So, they asked me to go to Atlanta, pay for the gas, and buy them meals as well. I am sure it was because I was a planner and frugal and seemed likely to be the easy target.

But I had something else in mind.

A little unsure of myself, I went to my head football coach for his thoughts and encouragement on attending the tryout camp. He quickly shuttled me into his office and closed the door.

"Robert," he said, "you're a good athlete, but not a great athlete. You've worked your butt off for us, and I appreciate that. You're fast, but not fast enough. You have good hands, but not great hands. You have this, but not that . . ." He stood in front of me moving his hands up and down like weights on the scales of justice—appropriate, I guess, since he was making such a show of judging my ability.

"Just let me be honest with you. . . ."

I was speechless. I had asked for his thoughts and encouragement. I certainly didn't expect a laundry list of my shortcomings!

"If you go—and you're certainly free to go—you'll not do very well. These tryouts are all about speed. You'll come in last, or close to last. You'll come back dejected. I know you're getting ready to graduate from college, so why don't you just move on?"

Wow, what an encouraging session!

The wind had been knocked out of me. I wanted to prove him wrong and go to the tryouts. But deep down, I believed everything he had said. At that precise moment, I realized football was over for me. Finding my teammates, I let them know I was not going to Atlanta after all. I didn't go to the tryouts because I thought my head coach was looking after my best interests.

And that was the end of it. All those football games from peewee through high school to college had just come to an abrupt end.

I was bothered by the way everything had turned out—until the guys asked me to go to Atlanta with them—knowing that those "backyard Super Bowl games" with the neighborhood kids were just dreams never to come true. I realized through all of my surgeries and rehab that my chances of advancing to the next level—as I had been allowed to four years earlier—and playing pro ball weren't going to materialize. I had to put those thoughts out of my head and get back to enjoying what was left of my UNA days.

Playing football after college? Get real!

I was only a month away from graduation. Campus was buzzing, hormones flowed, spring had sprung, and freedom loomed large.

One of the more fun events of late spring was a campus-wide Superstars contest sponsored by the sorority council to find out who was the best athlete at UNA. This was a local "knock-off" of the nationally televised Superstars contest, which had real athletes participating.

Need proof positive that not everyone looks after your best interests?

My own fraternity didn't ask their favorite football jock to be their Superstar contestant. Instead, they asked Tony Sexton, the younger brother of Tobin Sexton, a former teammate as well. Tony was a good athlete, but I knew I would outperform him in most of the events. But it looked like I would be watching from the stands. At the last minute, the ZTA sorority asked me to represent them.

The Superstars competition had seven events. The total scores from all the events—bowling, basketball free throw, hundred-yard dash, weightlifting, a golf long-drive contest, an obstacle course, and the rope climb—were combined to select the ultimate Superstar on campus. You had to participate in six of the seven events.

In the middle of the Superstar competition, adrenaline flowing, I was interrupted by a student breathless from having run across campus. I had no idea why he would want to talk to me.

"Coach Bill Baker," he said, referring to my offensive coordinator and pointing toward Flowers Hall, the athletic compound on campus. The kid took a minute to catch his breath, hands on knees. "He sent me to find you. There's a scout here from the Dallas Cowboys who wants to run you through some trials. Get your butt over to the athletic facility. QUICK!"

No problem!

It was an easy decision between the Superstars competition and my tryout with the Dallas Cowboys. I wanted to do well in the Superstars contest in front of my peers and felt like I had something to prove because I was the underdog one more time in my final athletic event as a student at UNA. But getting an opportunity to play professional football *is* every kid's dream. I had planned on skipping the rope climb but was allowed to skip the hundred-yard dash instead.

4.6

His name was Walt Yaworski, one of a handful of contract scouts around the country who assisted the Cowboys in locating new talent. Yaworski lived in Tennessee and had been around the block, hanging around small-college football programs watching UNA players like me for several years and getting the inside angle on hidden talent. He had a reputation for finding players who had flown under the radar and promoting them to the Cowboys (in fact, years after I met him, he was instrumental in touting a guy out of the University of Florida who was thought to be too slow to be successful, a running back by the name of Emmitt Smith).

I had met Yaworski before, and he seemed genuinely interested in me as a player. As I was on my way to the meeting on the field, I couldn't help but wonder how this was all going to play out.

What will he ask me?

What does a profootball tryout consist of?

What is Mr. Yaworski's role within the Cowboys organization and how can he help me to fulfill my dream of getting to the next level?

I was also thinking about my own inadequacies.

I know I'm not as fit as I could be. Will he know that and still give me a chance?

If I can only get this opportunity, I know I can get in great shape. I'll work hard, just wait and see.

Will he buy that?

Is this a hollow promise I am making to myself because I underprepared and spent the last four months enjoying life with my FIJI fraternity brothers?

You know the drill. No atheists in foxholes. People will make any rash promise to get an opportunity—or to postpone the inevitable.

The hard part is making good on those promises.

Turns out, the only thing Mr. Yaworski wanted to know was how fast I was. Period. Exactly what my head coach had told me about the Atlanta tryout. Speed is king in the NFL.

Forty yards isn't a long way to run—unless your professional future depends on it.

On the field, my first time for the forty-yard dash was 4.6 seconds—the fastest I had ever been timed in my life.

"You're not supposed to be that fast," Yaworski chuckled, rechecking his stopwatch. I laughed with him. He had a face like an old catcher's mitt, and the well-earned lines made it hard for him to hide his emotions.

"In fact, you can't be that fast. We've been tracking you for the past two years, and your speed was our only concern."

"Well, Mr. Yaworski, you don't understand," I told him, still breathing hard from the effort. "I've been training for this my whole life. All I need is an opportunity to make the Cowboys."

He didn't believe that. Why should he? Every promising young athlete would say the same thing. I probably sounded like Eddie Haskell from *Leave It to Beaver*.

While I caught my breath, I watched Yaworski retrace the route I'd run, step by step. He was measuring it again, thinking that he'd only paced off thirty-five yards the first time around.

"Sure enough," he said when he got to the starting line. "You ran forty."

Then he made me turn around and run in the other direction, because he thought the first run might have been wind-aided.

For good measure, he made me do it a third time.

By the time I was done, my lungs were burning—with effort, sure, but also with the adrenaline that had been coursing through my body since a wide-eyed student had told me I was about to undergo an impromptu professional tryout.

And every time: 4.6.

I'd never been timed faster than 4.8 prior to that day.

Had my speed increased, or had force of will carried me along?

Don't know, don't care!

My speed was locked in, at least for the upcoming draft, and I was fast enough to be a bona fide candidate.

After we chatted for a few minutes about my playing days at UNA and what positions I might play if I were drafted, Yaworski went into a coach's film room and watched four hours of film on my last two seasons.

With that glimmer of hope, I returned to the Superstars contest and won three of the next five events. In fact, I won the whole thing.

The final event was a rope climb, firefighter-like. I had never climbed a rope in my life. In fact, for four years I had walked by that rope climb and thought how tough it looked. The rope extended from the ground up to the top of the Flowers Hall gym some forty feet high. I was not afraid of heights—I just didn't want to have to climb that rope. I was not planning on participating in this event because I thought I could not do it. Now, after I had skipped the hundred-yard dash because of my try-out, the competition's final event was upon us. I watched the other contestants climb. I was the last contestant, feeling pulled like taffy between "I've never climbed this rope before or any rope for that matter" and "I've got to win this event to win the competition."

So what did I do?

I climbed the rope faster than anybody else, won the rope climb, won the event, won the competition, and the rest is history.

Of course, I gloated.

I stood on the platform in front of the entire campus and thanked the ZTA sorority for believing in me as I stared down my FIJI brothers for not sponsoring me.

After taking my bows, I ran across campus to see Yaworski, who had finished watching my game films and studying my ability in the kind of detail—and with an eye for weakness—that only scouts can.

Was I willing to block?

Was I willing to sacrifice myself and make a catch in a crowd?

Could I run great patterns consistently?

Did I take plays off?

He was also focusing on my weaknesses and deciding whether or not his team could rely on me as a player.

When he had finished watching the footage, he came out of the office and shook my hand.

"We'll be in touch," he said. That was it. For once, I couldn't read his response.

What did he mean? At that moment, I didn't know what to think. My coach had already dismissed my chances a month before, so why should I think a professional team had a real interest in me?

On his way out of the room, Yaworski turned back toward me. "You ran extremely well today, Robert. And you obviously can catch."

After a brief pause, he added, "You just might fit into our plans."

Red Zone Rules

Know Your Fans

Find your genuine supporters—the people you've identified as real leaders—and work with them.

In my first three years in college at the University of North Alabama, Coach Richie Gaskell offered that kind of support. He told me my hands were fine, but I had to increase my speed. Then he coached me on exactly how to do that.

"Be coachable," Coach Gaskell says. "That means being willing to change, practicing hard, and listening to your coaches when they instruct you on improving your play. Willingness is the secret quality that coaches admire. It shows you're flexible and can adapt to new situations, new plays, and new opportunities. Every player loves to practice what they're good at. But the only way to improve is to be willing to practice what you're not good at, even when it looks like you're failing."

If you're the underdog, you've got to give your all—every day, every play—and you'll never have a reason to look back on any performance with regrets. Be an every-day, every-play kind of player.

What do the 1980 United States hockey team, the 1983 North Carolina State basketball team, and the 2008 New York Giants have in common?

They pulled off the greatest upsets in sports history, sure.

But what else do the players on those teams share?

A passion for the sport and a willingness to work for that one shot—thousands and thousands of hours of dedication for a single moment.

They were ready when the time came. Will you be?

Buck the Odds

Bruce Huther, a former Cowboys teammate, knows what it's like to be the underdog.

"There's a tendency with teammates, coaches, and your friends to look at the odds of your making the team and leading you to believe it isn't going to happen," Bruce told me once.

"You have to be mentally tough. How do you believe in yourself? You've just got to do it. That's one of the mental parts of this culture: believing in yourself regardless of what anyone else says is probably the toughest part, pushing through their beliefs about you."

When young, we are naïve and believe that others, specifically coaches, are looking out for our best interests. That's not always true. Some well-meaning people may not be looking after your best interests.

You're the only one who can do that!

Make this motto a part of your success DNA: *"If it's going to be, it's up to me."*

Hit the Books

In the spring of 1978, I achieved one of the goals I set for myself when I arrived on campus four years earlier—to graduate on time with my class. In hindsight, the accomplishment was bittersweet. As I look back on my college days, I realize that I missed important honors and recognitions in college because I didn't set *high enough* goals for myself. One of those goals should have been to graduate with honors, which I missed narrowly. But I arrived on campus with no study skills and even less of an idea of what I wanted to do when I graduated. One of my other goals was to not make a D or an F throughout college. Another goal was to make sure it was my effort and not cheating on tests as I had done in high school trying to just get by.

Football got me to the University of North Alabama. Avoiding Ds and Fs kept me motivated.

By the second semester, my grades had improved, and by my sophomore year, I was on the Dean's List, where I stayed for five of the next six semesters. If my goal had been to graduate with honors, I could have accomplished it. But graduating with honors wasn't part of my thought process at the time.

Don't let *if I had only known* become part of your vocabulary.

Do your homework when you enter into a new adventure.

Find out your options and get all of the required information. For example, you'll see in this book how valuable it was for me as the underdog to learn to listen closely to an NFL veteran's advice, "Watch people. Listen to others."

The only way to know is by stretching, exploring, and learning. Imagine playing for the Dallas Cowboys, missing a play, and saying to the coach, "If only I had known." You'd be gone before you had time to change out of your uniform. Now imagine that your job in life is to know—and when you don't know, you find out.

Knowing leads to expertise, which leads to exceptional achievement in the making.

2

Top Dog

Cowboys

Texas Stadium and the Cowboys headquarters in Dallas were a beehive of activity. Even after the impressive win in January over the Broncos, Cowboys management—including team architects Tex Schramm and Gil Brandt—wouldn't let the team get complacent.

Known for their work ethic, this unique triumvirate included Tom Landry, the fedora-wearing football genius who had come to Dallas in 1960 and eventually led the Cowboys for twenty-nine seasons. The team was always desperate (an odd but appropriate word to use for world champions) to improve their chances of repeating.

In the coming months, the Cowboys would draft twelve players and bring in another eighty jocks and journeymen to participate in summer camp. Every one of them, of course, was convinced that he could make the team. Those ninety-two players—along with the forty-five returning players from the 1978 team, all of whom already had big-game experience in the

NFL—would compete for a spot on the Dallas Cowboys roster. There were 137 players for forty-five roster spots.

Hardly good odds for the new guys coming into camp. Training camp would trim most of them (many of them quickly, like the injured and the sick at the back of a pack of antelope), and the final roster cuts would come in late August—just in time for the season opener against the tough Baltimore Colts and Bert Jones, their talented veteran quarterback.

Underdog

Thanks to my head coach and his advice that I was too slow to play in the NFL, I was sure that I would graduate and go into the insurance business. Five days after meeting with Walt Yaworski and impressing him with my speed (or at least showing him that I wasn't as slow as he thought I was), I received a letter from the Dallas Cowboys.

"We're contemplating drafting you. Fill out these papers," the letter stated simply.

And by the way: "Who's your agent?"

Agent? I didn't have an agent!

Did I need an agent? I filled out the requested forms wondering if my lack of an agent might hurt my chances, make me look like just another player who didn't know the ropes.

Three days later, I received another letter—this one generic and impersonal—and a glossy marketing piece that was a real letdown for a young guy dying to play for the team. Instead of showing real interest in me as a player, the materials reminded me of something that would be sent to a season-ticket holder. I knew who the Cowboys were, but I wasn't sure they knew who I was.

I started to doubt the whole scene.

Were they playing with me now?

Was this the way it went for every guy on the bubble waiting to hear from an NFL team?

I felt suspended in time, half-sick at waiting for news.

The NFL draft didn't hold the same significance it does now, with wall-to-wall coverage, television cameras in players' homes, rabid fans in Radio City Music Hall celebrating their team's pick and booing an opponent's, cell phones chirping, agents playing the angles, and multimillion dollar signing bonuses in the balance.

In 1978, the two days of the draft weren't televised, and the public knew little of what happened until they read about it in the local newspaper or saw it on the evening news. The first day came and went without any correspondence from the Cowboys—or any other team, for that matter. My parents called to ask me what was going on, and I couldn't give them any more news than they already had.

The next day was business as usual. In fact, instead of worrying about the draft, I began to prepare for my college finals. Coming down to my last two tests in college felt great. An answer from the Cowboys would have made those tests easier to prepare for, I thought, and in the middle of my daydreams and half-studying a business textbook, the phone rang.

"Robert. Cornell Green here." The voice was crisp, matter-of-fact, and I had no idea who that was on the other end of the line. "I've just arrived in Atlanta from Dallas. I'm driving to Florence. I don't know how long it will take me, but I'm assuming I'll get there around seven. You'll be there?"

Who is Cornell Green?

"OK, Mr. Green. That sounds great. What are you coming to see me about?"

"We've just finished the draft, and while we thought about drafting you in the twelfth round, we decided to fill another need."

"I understand. The draft's over, huh? I'll look forward to meeting you when you arrive in Florence." My heart sank. I wasn't going to be playing in the NFL after all. But I couldn't for the life of me figure why Cornell Green—whoever he was— would want to see me in Florence.

"No, no, I'm coming up to sign you," he corrected. "My only reason for making this trip is to offer you a free agent contract to become a part of the Dallas Cowboys. I'm driving to Florence now. And I won't be leaving until I have your signature on a contract."

A contract. A contract. A contract. I kept repeating Green's final words until they sank in.

A contract!

Football was back in my life!

I'd never felt elation like that. I didn't breathe for about two minutes, and I couldn't get my heart to stop racing. Here I was about to become a professional athlete, and I felt like I had just run a marathon without moving from my chair.

I called my parents and told them the news. They were excited and wanted me to let them know as soon as I had "inked the deal" (my dad, the serial entrepreneur, read way too many business magazines; I reminded them that it was just a free-agent contract, not a lease on Peachtree Plaza). When my dad asked me how studying was going, I laughed and made some remark about finding time to study that night.

Right!

I was at my apartment faking a sincere desire to study and not being able to concentrate, but who could blame me? I was having trouble keeping a lid on my excitement for five hours until Cornell Green arrived in town.

Mark Spry helped talk me down. We wondered what it would be like to play for the Cowboys. Mark, who knew his sports inside and out, explained that Cornell Green had a reputation first as a basketball player from Oklahoma City. He went on to play at Utah State University and became a three-time All-Conference player before signing with the Cowboys as a free agent in 1962. So Cornell knew something about the process that I was about to go through—and he had been fortunate enough to spend thirteen seasons with the team he loved.

I was about to meet a Cowboy star who had paid his dues.

An hour and a half later, I received another phone call. I answered the phone thinking it was my sister Vicki, wanting to congratulate me, as she has always been one of my biggest supporters. Instead, it was a booming male voice, another person I didn't recognize.

"Hi, Robert. We haven't spoken before. I'm Bill Jones, with the Seattle Seahawks. I'm in Birmingham, driving up to Florence, and I'll be there around six-thirty or seven." He spoke quickly, and I'm not sure that I even responded until he had finished. I heard what he was saying, but I was having trouble processing.

Two hours ago, I thought I would never play another down of football. Now, if I was hearing Bill Jones correctly, I'd just gotten my second offer that day to sign with an NFL team.

I remember Mark sitting on the couch just looking at me, worried that something was wrong—so Jones took that as permission to continue.

"I'm coming to sign you to a free agent contract. You weren't drafted. We were thinking about drafting you in the final round, but we want to sign you to a free agent contract instead."

A familiar story. Thought about drafting me, but. . . .

I think I thanked Jones for calling and hung up. And for a couple of minutes, I just sat there in the chair, numb.

I have two scouts coming to Florence, Alabama. That probably hasn't ever happened.

I don't know what to do.

Sure enough, I found out later that two scouts had never come to Florence, Alabama, to sign a UNA player to a free agent contract. In fact, only a handful of players had ever been drafted or signed as a free agent, and none had made a pro football team since Harlon Hill in 1953.

Having two pro scouts in town with the same intentions seemed special, at least to me.

But who had the slightest idea how it would all play out?

Negotiation Station

Cornell Green arrived in Florence and checked into the Holiday Inn. When he called, he asked me to meet him in the hotel lobby.

Two minutes later, the phone rang again. It was Bill Jones, the Seahawks scout.

"I just pulled into Dale's Restaurant. What's the chance of your coming here to have dinner with me?"

"I'll be there in thirty minutes," I told him in a panic.

I sent Mark to meet Jones. I went to the Holiday Inn to see Green.

Give Cornell credit, he was to the point. He gave me the Cowboys song and dance in under twenty minutes. Let's face it, he was a salesman with a great product, and he knew it. If he had just stood there and held out the contract, I would have said the same thing.

I was sold on the Cowboys.

"Mr. Green, you know I want to play for you. I'd be crazy not to. You know what an opportunity this is." I must have hesitated a beat too long.

"But . . ." There was an edge to Green's face. He might not have been in playing shape and hadn't strapped on a helmet in a few years, but he took care of himself, the kind of guy who looked like he could drive a nail with his forehead (and probably had at some point).

"But right now, I need to do one other thing."

Green didn't blink. And he didn't speak. It was more than a little nerve-wracking.

"I have to go to Dale's Restaurant, just around the corner. I've got to see a scout from the Seahawks. I should have told you when you got here, but it all happened . . . too fast."

From Green, nothing.

"He told me he wants to sign me to a free-agent contract."

I'll never forget Green's next move—the best thing any salesperson could have done.

"Well, why don't we just go together?" He knew that if I was out of his sight, the guy could have signed me to a contract. Hell, I didn't know whether I was coming or going at that point. I probably would have signed a contract to wash uniforms for the Cowboys training camp if he had offered.

No, if Green didn't return to Dallas with my signature, that would have been a wasted trip and ten hours of flying and driving for no reason—even though he was just signing some kid with a little bit of heart who may or may not pan out.

When Green and I got to the restaurant, I introduced myself to the Seahawks scout and told him right away that I was about to sign with the Cowboys.

He nodded. When it came to NFL teams, the Seahawks, who had only been in existence for two seasons at that point, would always have a hard time competing with the Cowboys for talent. They did use the same scouting combine with the Cowboys to locate talent, which is why they even showed up in the first place. They had a great young receiver in Steve Largent and a fine quarterback in the lefty Jim Zorn, but they were no match for the Cowboys.

"Well, I understand," Jones said. I could tell he wasn't a bad salesman himself, just kind of letting things come to him. "But may I at least offer you a deal?"

As it turned out, he offered me more money.

Here I was, twenty-one years old, knowing nothing about the world—and even less about negotiating a contract with two NFL teams at the same time—and I had the upper hand. I kept going from one table to the other.

Every time I changed tables, I was offered $2,500 more.

Hey, this was fun. I could do this for a long time.

The Seattle scout had to put me on the phone with the player personnel director in Seattle for approval of the next $2,500. Most of the money was slated for the future years of the contract, which meant I'd get none of it if I didn't make the team. As young as I was, I observed with interest that Green could make such decisions on his own authority, while the scout from Seattle had to call somebody else.

Green eventually tired of the game and wanted to eat the steak he had ordered. No doubt the Seattle player personnel director didn't think I'd be that difficult a fish to land, and the longer the game went on, the more flustered Jones and his higher-up on the other end of the line got.

Green was cool, professional, and patient with me as I went back and forth. At some point, though, enough was enough.

"Robert, let me be real honest with you," Green said with a hint of a sigh in his voice. "Did I mention earlier that we're the World Champions and beat Denver in Super Bowl XII? You're well aware of this, right?"

Why would you even have to mention it? Of course, I know who won the Super Bowl this year!

What he said next was probably the most truthful line he spoke all night.

"Well, there's a chance—a good one—coming in as a free agent with the Cowboys that you might not make the team. The money in years two and three won't mean anything to you if you're released this summer."

He took another bite of steak and let that sink in. While I was contemplating this, he told me the steak was one of the best rib eyes he had ever had. Coming from a true-blue Cowboy, this statement was certainly a compliment to my favorite restaurant. He then interrupted my thoughts.

"So we're talking about the money for this year only. And if the Cowboys cut you, there are twenty-seven other teams—including the Seahawks and your friend Mr. Jones over there—who would be interested in making you a free-agent offer."

I nodded.

"But let's face it. If you get cut by the Seattle Seahawks, your butt is on a bus back to Columbus, Georgia, before you can order another cup of coffee. You understand what I'm saying?"

He had set the hook.

"Yes sir. I hear you loud and clear."

Green played Salesmanship 101 well—sell your strengths while letting your prospect understand the consequences of "purchasing" an inferior product. He put a small seed of doubt in my mind, and I was completely sold.

In Green's case, I bought the product. The whole enchilada.

"Mr. Green, I'm done negotiating. Let me go tell Mr. Jones that I'm going to be a Dallas Cowboy."

When the negotiations were finished and I could take a breath and relax, I looked at the tables and saw that I had ordered two huge rib eye steaks, my favorite as well. I hadn't eaten a bite of either one of them because I was negotiating the whole time—and feeling more than a little sick to my stomach. My excitement numbed any hunger I might have had. Nor did I eat the rest of the evening. Leaving a Dale's steak—let alone two—on the table isn't something I had done before or since. In fact, I only eat steaks today that have been marinated in Dale's Steak Sauce because of my memories of Dale's Restaurant in Florence during my years at UNA.

When the negotiations were complete, Green asked if we could go somewhere, grab a drink, and sign the paperwork. The restaurant was closing and we needed to relocate.

"This is a dry county, Mr. Green. We'll have to drive to 'The Line' in Tennessee, our after-hours entertainment at UNA. Or I could send one of my friends to the local bootlegger and we could go to my apartment. The choices aren't great, but what he has is pretty good."

"Call him. I'm thirsty."

Green and I drove over to my apartment. He began weaving stories about making the Cowboys as a free agent, Coach Tom Landry, the excitement of playing in the NFL, and becoming a mainstay on the team.

A half hour later Mark returned from the bootlegger's house with the brown package in hand. We opened the Canadian Mist whiskey and poured each other generous drinks.

Green offered a toast to my first job out of college. "Robert, you're on your way. The hardest work of your life is about to hit you like a freight train. If you believe it, you can achieve it. I did and I believe you can, too."

And at that moment, I had never believed in anything more in my whole life.

I didn't know if Green was about to begin preaching or not, but I was mesmerized by his words. The alcohol continued to flow until we had one final drink and I could tell Cornell needed some sleep.

"I've got three more players to sign tomorrow," Green said, getting up off the couch. "Please drive me back to my hotel."

I was quite pleased with myself that I was his first "close," because that meant I was his first target as well.

When he had been safely delivered, Mark and I stayed up most of the night talking and phoning. I couldn't believe what had happened in the space of a few hours.

What in the hell have I just done?

Waking up the next morning, never having cracked a book open the previous night, I floated into my final exams not caring what I made on the tests. I had high Bs going in and finished both with Cs.

Who cared?

I was headed to Dallas to try to find a spot on America's Team.

College was over, and I would be walking down the graduation aisle in the UNA gym with a nice piece of paper in my hands to match the contract I signed.

I'm not sure what came over me right then, but I had a burning desire to take my contract to the athletic offices and tell the head coach to kiss my ass.

I didn't. Maybe my upbringing as a Southern gentleman took over. Or maybe I understood that, in some weird way, he had helped light the fire that would fuel my success. Making the Cowboys would be my vengeance and my KMA statement more boldly that even speaking it.

In fact, I didn't tell anyone about my contract. Not even the Florence, Alabama, media found out until I was already in camp. I had just accomplished my goal, being offered an opportunity to advance to the next level, and this chapter of my life was that next bold step forward. I really didn't want anyone to know about this until after I had made the team. No parades, no fanfare, just business as usual. I had my diploma in hand. Proof positive that goals could be achieved with proper effort, attitude, and paying the right price to achieve any goal I set. I would figure out the rest at a later time.

The next morning, as I contemplated my next choice in life, I began to feel comfortable, even peaceful, about my direction, convinced that the signing ceremony in my apartment was something more than just ink on a piece of paper.

I will make this team.

I didn't know how, but I knew. Resolve swept over me like a flowing river.

I had set my goal—a spot on America's Team was in my sights—but how would I accomplish it?

Red Zone Rules

The Art of the Deal

When negotiating, remember whether you're the buyer or the seller. Many times, it's the buyer who sells the seller on their terms, not the other way around.

Stay honest, professional, and courteous during negotiations, but don't feel that you need to reveal everything. "Know when to hold 'em; know when to fold them," Kenny Rogers famously sang. Generally, the first one to put an offer on the table sets the bar for where the final price will land. See what they've got to offer you before you make your offer and your final decision. Weigh your options carefully, knowing that once you've made your decision, you'll never look back with regret. My father taught me this early on and I've lived it my entire life. Once you have made your decision, never look back. Also, never burn your bridges—you may need to cross that river again at some point.

Whatever your particular "game" may be—whether it's football or some other sport, your chosen career, a family— always be willing to play the game, to immerse yourself in the moment. Give it your absolute best. Know the players around you. Show your willingness to adapt to changing circumstances. Watch how everybody works together, and don't be shy about jumping in to help the team.

Above all, trust your gut. Intuition can be a valuable guide, but you've got to visualize every conceivable move that can or will be made.

Imagine that you're in a giant, real-life chess game.

When you make a move, anticipate what your opponent will do in return.

Think things through carefully—and then let your instincts take over.

A Time and a Place

After all these years, Cornell Green still remembers the night he signed me on to play with the Cowboys. What an honor for me to know the gentleman I discovered Cornell Green to be.

Thanks to him, I got my big break.

I've had a great relationship over the years with Cornell, and I asked him what he remembered about our first meeting.

"Robert was a very sincere kid. He said, 'Well, Mr. Green, I can't sign with you right now because I've got to talk to the Seattle Seahawks and they're waiting on me at a restaurant.' I told him, 'Fine. I'll just take you to the restaurant.'

"So we both went to the restaurant, and I saw the Seattle Seahawk scout sitting over there, and I got a table on the other end of the restaurant. Then Robert ordered a steak over there and a steak over here. Two steaks was a lot to chew on.

"What he was doing, which was very smart of him, was playing both ends. I don't believe he had any idea what he was doing, but it was smart. This whole dinner thing lasted three to four hours."

Training camp was a world away from sleepy little Florence, Alabama, and when I got there, I was glad to see a familiar face, even if I had only met Cornell once and really appreciated the hours we talked that night.

"In training camp he showed me that he was a very good football player. I thought he was a great kid. I thought he was very levelheaded. It's very rare for a free agent to make it. But it happens," Cornell said. "You don't have to be the strongest guy out there. You don't have to be the biggest guy. You just have to be athletic, with speed, and have what it takes to play the position that you're going to play."

Later, I saw Cornell on the sidelines.

"Hey, Cornell." I started over to shake his hand and to catch up with him. I felt as though we had already established some camaraderie after our meeting in Florence.

I was surprised and a little hurt when he just nodded his head, and turned and walked the other way.

Well, that's not the same Cornell I saw in the restaurant or my apartment that night.

But that was the image Cornell wanted me to have, and he cultivated it wisely.

He wasn't going to acknowledge the fact that we spent an evening talking and drinking when he came to Florence to sign me—until I had made the team.

The message was clear: "These are the rules, Underdog. Get with the game!"

Get the Lay of the Land

Bill Baker, my offensive coordinator at UNA, knows a little something about football. He's been a scout for four different NFL teams over the last twenty years, and he's seen a lot of talent come and go.

"As UNA's offensive coordinator, I could count on Robert to be on the field when he was needed and to execute the play I had called. He was an outstanding individual and a good football player for UNA. When the Cowboys organization sent their scouting sheets to UNA's athletic department, I filled out those papers on Robert so the Cowboys would follow up. At that time, the Cowboys were one of the most innovative teams as far as recruiting and scouting. The Cowboys' scouts dug and searched to find a diamond in the rough, even in Division II schools. Robert was one of those diamonds.

"It's still a huge jump, a huge battle for a Division II player. He just immediately has strikes against him, because of the competition level. That is why such a great success story like Robert's can inspire other college diamonds-in-the-rough to go for their big dream."

Everyone who's paid attention to the NFL over the last decade knows the story of Kurt Warner, who went from little Northern Iowa University to a job as a grocery clerk to Super Bowl champ and multiple-MVP of the NFL while with the Saint Louis Rams.

Stories like Warner's don't happen often, but they do happen.

When you know the lay of the land.

Exorcise Your Mind

Our minds play far too many tricks on us, usually more negatively than positively. Chasing out those demons is a constant battle when pushing yourself beyond what you and others think you are capable of. But it is your internal belief that you can accomplish far more than others give you credit for or believe you can that should drive you to dig deep in your soul—and keep pushing yourself beyond the limits we often place on ourselves.

3

The Plan

Freshman Year (Spring 1975)

When I got to college, I couldn't bench press 150 pounds. I couldn't do twenty chin-ups. I didn't know what it was really like to get hit—really hit hard—on the football field. I had only played one season of high school football where I actually saw game-action. Today, we would say I had a steep learning curve to negotiate. When I showed up at the University of North Alabama, the response was more direct: "Son, you're just not ready to play college football."

To make matters worse, I'd been injured during spring training my freshman year in college—with little college action under my belt—which resulted in major surgery on my left knee. As difficult as it was to accept that I'd be out of football for a while, I learned a few valuable lessons during my rehab. One had to do with listening to my body. During the rehab on my left knee, I pushed my body past the point of pain, putting so much strain on the healthy parts on my healthy leg—the "good knee," as Coach Gaskell referred to it—that that knee required surgery in the fall of my sophomore year.

More rehab, more lessons learned.

I spent about fifteen weeks on crutches, going up and down UNA's stairs with heavy book bags, wondering about my future in football. Many times, I would look around for someone to help me with the books, especially when it rained. Those were the dark days, but I couldn't have succeeded mentally without the physical challenges that forced me to reassess where I was and where I wanted to be. I overheard a few of the fraternity guys one afternoon as I was trucking to class say, "Is he ever going to be off crutches?" You could say that my popularity and my self-esteem sank to new lows as I trudged across campus day after day on crutches.

A funny thing happened on the way to practice my junior year. I went into the weight room, where linemen spent most of their time grunting and sweating and shouting at each other to get one more rep. The receivers watched in awe, like witnesses to a circus sideshow finale, where all the strongmen come out and pose for the audience.

Today, the idea that receivers could perform at their peak without extensive weight-room conditioning would be absurd. But in the mid-1970s, position players focused more on their skills than their physiques. When I saw what the linemen were doing—and after my own experiences in rehab—it occurred to me that strength was a key to success.

The first time I went into the weight room, my junior fall, I was stunned that I could bench-press 250 pounds. The increase in strength was an unintended result of the knee injuries. I'd never focused my training on my upper body because I had spent so much time strengthening my legs through lifting weights, running, and isometrics. But I had gained tremendous upper body strength from relying on the crutches twice in the past year.

At the time, I didn't want to lift weights—too much work! But Newton's law is a tough one to do an end-run around: "For every action, there is an equal and opposite reaction." I believe one thing further. For every reaction, there is either a consequence or a benefit. And the knee injuries had, in a funny way, given me the secret to conditioning that would be so important to my later success.

When I had my first knee surgery, I thought, *That's just a setback.*

Another year, another knee surgery. *Another temporary setback.*

As a junior, though, I was a starter with two knee operations on his résumé. The coaches were afraid of my getting hurt again and wasting the scholarship they'd given me. I didn't want to let them down, certainly, but more importantly, I didn't want my football career to come to a screeching halt.

And in the end, I proved to myself and my coaches that the investment they had made in me would pay dividends and that I could withstand the punishment of an entire football season without further injury to my knees. Of course, the hits and in game action to my shoulders, hips, neck, and other body parts hurt like hell every Sunday morning after a tough game.

I led the league in receiving yards as a junior, having hardly played as a freshman or a sophomore. Then our coaching staff—including my mentor Coach Gaskell and Mickey Andrews, the future legendary defensive coordinator at Florida State—was fired and a new coaching staff took over with an eye toward "rebuilding." I wanted to win football games, but I never did find common ground with the new coach—the same one who encouraged me not to go to the Atlanta tryouts after my senior season. (In fact, he spoke to my date at the senior athletic banquet for the team, but didn't speak to me or acknowledge me in any way, nor did I receive a single award.)

When I was voted All-Conference my senior season, it was by the media, not my own coaches.

Synchronicity

I'm not even certain where I heard it for the first time, but the saying stuck with me: "If you chase two rabbits, they'll both escape." Relevant to my Southern upbringing, I suppose, since I knew a lot of hunters and outdoorsmen, but really on the mark when it came to my challenge to become an NFL player.

As an underdog, I learned perseverance and awareness. Confidence breeds competence, and one of the most effective coping tools anyone can cultivate—athletes, businesspeople, students, parents—is tunnel vision. Tunnel vision occurs when a goal becomes so real in your body and mind that you see it everywhere. Maybe you could call it extreme focus, which is why I thought of the idea of chasing two rabbits. Sometimes we get so caught up in the world around us, being pulled a hundred different ways at the same time, that we can't commit to doing one thing *really well.*

Once I became obsessed with being a Cowboy, though, and bought into the idea with all my being, I started to become aware of things around me that I had missed before.

For one, the generic letter I received just before the draft—the one that forced me to question the whole process. The letter read, in part, "Thanks for your interest in the Dallas Cowboys organization. We look forward to talking with you in the future." Not a very promising introduction. But enclosed with the letter was a media guide sent only to rookies—though I hadn't known that at the time and had initially felt disappointed in what I felt was an impersonal letter.

Several weeks after I signed my free-agent contract, I sat down and really read the stories in that marketing piece about

Cliff Harris and Drew Pearson making the team as free agents themselves. Drew commented that what helped him make the team was going to Dallas in the summer prior to camp and working out at the Cowboys practice facility, a visit that helped to introduce him to the mindset of a professional football player.

Drew came from the University of Tulsa, a school about the size of UNA. In fact, UT was the smallest Division I school in America, and the only reason Drew was able to get noticed was through hard work. Neither the most talented nor the fastest receiver with the Cowboys, Drew, like all the greats, made his job look easy enough that the casual observer had no idea how much dedication he had given to his craft.

Drew will always be known for some of the more dramatic plays in Cowboys history, including his over-the-top reception—remembered by Cowboys fans simply as the "Hail Mary"—against the Minnesota Vikings in a 1975 divisional play-off game. Down 14–10 with twenty-four seconds left in the game, Roger Staubach scrambled out of trouble and threw a desperation pass fifty yards downfield. Drew, whose defender had fallen on the play, trapped the ball on his hip (he admitted later that he wasn't even sure he had caught the pass) and backed into the end zone for the winning score. Vikings fans were incensed when the Cowboys escaped with a 17–14 win and moved on to the NFC Championship game—where they dismantled the Los Angeles Rams—before losing to the Pittsburgh Steelers in Super Bowl X.

After the Vikings game, Roger coined the phrase that's become commonplace in the NFL when he told a reporter that, before throwing the pass, "I closed my eyes and said a Hail Mary."

A knack for the big play put Drew, a three-time Pro Bowl selection, in the first rank of receivers to ever play the game, his career statistics speak for themselves: 489 catches for 7,822 yards and 50 touchdowns. He deserves to be in the Hall of Fame—an honor that has, unfortunately, eluded him up till now.

So when I saw how similar my own background was to Drew's, I knew the media guide I received was a sign of sorts. If I hadn't seen what guys like Drew and Cliff (who was from Ouachita Baptist University in Arkadelphia, Arkansas, not a football powerhouse) had gone through, I never would have thought that a kid coming out of UNA had any chance in hell of making the Cowboys roster. Those guys showed me it was possible, especially for someone willing to put in the work.

When I read that, I set intermediate goals necessary to accomplish my *ultimate* goal—to make the team. I had to be invited as a participant in the summer training session, plain and simple, or I wouldn't have the same feeling or understanding about the people and the process. What really caught my attention was the fact that the Cowboys extended invitations to a select few to work out in Dallas with the other veterans prior to training camp. So I set that as my next intermediate goal. I would have to impress the scouts enough in the rookie orientation that they would select me to come to Dallas to work out for the summer.

I knew I could benefit a great deal from knowing exactly what to expect when I got to Dallas, so I called Harlon Hill, a source of inspiration for me. His story, along with the letter and the media guide I had gotten from the Cowboys, was exactly what I needed to get me moving in the right direction.

Red Zone Rules

Trust Your Intuition

The underdog can't deny his intuition. People might say that my confidence about knowing I would make the World Champions as a free agent smacked of arrogance. Believing with your heart, though, isn't arrogant, it's the seat of intuition, the place where confidence comes from and dreams are born.

Arrogance would be bragging. Confidence is knowing the facts in your heart and head and then acting upon those feelings until you accomplish your goals. I knew in my heart, mind, and soul that I would make the team. No ifs, ands, or buts—I was going to be a Dallas Cowboy.

Drew Pearson says, "I approached the game with intuition. Because of that, I had a lot of knowledge of what was going on out there. I could perceive things. I could feel things even before they would happen.

"I could anticipate how a defense was going to play, how a guy might come at me to tackle me. I had a good feel, that sixth sense. I was a quarterback in high school and part of college. So, that's how I approached the game, looked at things from a totally different perspective than a guy playing wide receiver or defensive end. Those guys might only have one perspective on a particular play. They may understand their roles very well, what it takes to help the team be successful.

"But when you're a quarterback, you have to see the game from an overall perspective and understand everybody's roles.

And that's how I looked at the game of football even when I stopped playing QB and started playing wide receiver."

The strong feeling Drew describes led me to set two new life-goals after signing the contract with Cornell Green. The first was to make the Cowboys. The second was to be awarded a game ball.

Intuition and the belief it spawned made me a very different person from just a month earlier, when my coach said my football career was over and I should move on.

Here's the bottom line: You're the only person who will look out for your own best interests and your plan. *No one* else will do it.

Take action.

Do the right thing.

If you want something badly enough, and you resolve in your mind to accomplish it, that goal should permeate your soul.

Trust your intuition and follow your feelings.

Before you commit to a task or a goal (what's a goal, really, but a series of tasks that will help you to reach the desired endpoint?), know exactly what you're getting into. Remember the old adage: "Be careful what you ask for. You just might get it." Research the good, the bad, and the ugly of the goal. Know what will be expected of you. Be prepared to change the goal once you know all the facts.

Tell yourself, "I will do whatever it takes." Then, and only then, will you accomplish your goal.

Learn to Take a Punch

Knowing how to set goals and mustering the effort to accomplish them were skills that I honed early in my college career. I can trace my decision to improve to several events.

In my late teen years, Dad owned a construction company, apartments, hotels, and other businesses. We had a family friend, Richard Smith. Richard should have accomplished more—

at least according to my youthful eyes—but he never got any significant breaks in life. He was a good man who just seemed to hop from one job to another always looking for his big break. He and I painted houses together and worked construction, typical summer jobs for a teen like me. Richard was the son-in-law of the man I was named after, Robert Hendrix. The Hendrix family and the Steeles are close to this day and always will be.

For six weeks during my senior year in high school, I worked with Richard, one of the most positive strugglers I'd ever been around. I haven't forgotten what he told me: "Never let something get the best of you. Never, ever get beat mentally. You can always overcome. You can always take it to the next level if you want to. Most people choose to let something get the best of them."

I listened intently as I was about to head off to football camp for my senior year of high-school football. These words were in my head as I was in summer camp, doing four-a-days—not the normal two-a-days—that every football player hated. So, for four practices a day—6:00 a.m., 10:00 a.m., 2:00 p.m., and 6:00 p.m.—the Hawks of Hardaway High spent one week in Moultrie, Georgia, growing up mentally, physically, and emotionally. We came back to town changed young men. Had it not been for Richard Smith, whose words I had to think about four times a day and throughout the night to just keep putting one foot in front of the other, I would not have made it through that grueling week. His words left a strong impression. I thought of Richard even as I left for Dallas on the eve of tackling the biggest challenge of my life.

What's Your Identity?

In football, one of the strongest predictors of success is how well a team knows its "identity"—that is, how to win games over the course of a long season and to situate the team for a successful play-off run.

Are we a high-flying passing team relying on offense to cover for a weak defense?

Are we a grinding offense scoring just enough to help out our stingy defense?

Are we a balanced team that can keep opponents off balance and win in a number of different ways?

It's the same in life. You'll always have to face and overcome adversity if you want to be successful. The ball won't always bounce your way. When it does, enjoy it. When it doesn't, know how you're going to respond.

Know your identity. Recognize who you are, what you are, where you are, and what you need to do to overcome adversity.

Then go out and do your job.

That's a major point for many naïve people in the world who trust everybody—and I'm probably one of the more trusting people. I've been burned in the past, having lost a lot of money trusting people who were only looking after their best interests all at my expense.

But because I never lost sight of my identity, I've learned from those mistakes and moved on.

Judging the Book by Its Cover

"Robert Steele was an undrafted free agent and certainly didn't look like a professional football player," Drew Pearson recalls.

"I was the same way when I came in 1973—six foot one, 165 pounds with no muscle, because I never lifted any weights in high school and never lifted weights in college. People took one look at me and said, 'This guy has no chance.' They laughed at me. They saw my skinny legs and my skinny upper body and assumed that I would be gone long before the season opened.

"Of course, I ended up proving them wrong.

"When I saw Robert Steele for the first time, I thought to myself, *Now I know what people thought of me*. Because I saw Robert and didn't give him any chance of making the team. Too skinny, too slow.

"Since he was a receiver, he was in my practice groups, doing all the things I did in training camp in the preseason, getting ready for the upcoming season. *There's no way this guy is going to make it*—I thought that all the time.

"But he was the Energizer Bunny out there, just kept working, doing what he had to do, kept his head down, and acted like he knew what the outcome was going to be. That must have impressed the coaches as much as it impressed the players. There's a sort of grudging admiration that comes from watching someone work so hard that it makes *you* tired.

"The difference wasn't what you saw on the outside, but what he was made of inside—the desire to prove people wrong. Beyond that, Robert was intelligent and had a plan.

"I think that was the biggest thing I had going for myself, too, the thing we had in common, knowledge and intelligence and a path to our goals. I always thought I could outsmart somebody or be smart enough to grasp the concepts thrown our way from Coach Landry and his new system. 'The intangibles,' they call it today. Just paying attention and working hard at the mental game gave us an edge that offset the physical shortcomings Robert and I might have had.

"Robert had that intelligence. He learned. He picked up the subtleties, watching me run my pass routes. He was smart enough to emulate the way I did things, but as camp progressed, I could see him starting to put his own flourishes on things, to begin to create an identity that the coaches paid attention to.

"When people judged our books by their covers—that is, took what they saw in us at face value—they could get burned."

4

Old School

Harlon's Story

Up till 1978, Harlon Hill was the only player from the University of North Alabama who had played professional football. Several other Lion alums had tried out for teams after Harlon, but none had ever made an NFL roster. Now, I had the opportunity to change that.

I came to know Harlon through his son Jerry—a UNA freshman receiver when I was a senior—and I helped Jerry adapt to college football. At the time, I thought his dad was just another high school coach in the area. I knew that Harlon had played pro football, but I didn't know the real importance of the Harlon Hill story.

The comfortable, small town of Florence, Alabama, was the home of Florence State Teacher's College in the early 1950s. Established as La Grange College in 1830, FSTC received funding in 1872 as a teachers' college and, in my freshman year 1974, became the University of North Alabama. It was probably the last place a professional football team would scout for new talent—until Harlon Hill came along.

As an offensive end, Harlon was named NAIA All-American in 1953, his senior year, and was drafted in 1954 by the Chicago Bears. After being honored as the NFL's Rookie of the Year, he was named the league's Most Valuable Player in 1955.

Talk about rising up from obscurity to become one of the most feared receivers in the NFL. Here was a guy from little Florence State Teachers College breaking into a league known for its ferocity and the grit and determination of its players, many of whom had come back from World War II to play professional football.

Harlon played eight seasons for the Bears before finishing his career with the Pittsburgh Steelers and the Detroit Lions. An ankle injury in 1962 cut Harlon's NFL career short. He went back to Alabama and taught and coached at Brooks High School, where he eventually became the head football coach and principal. In 1986, the first annual Harlon Hill Trophy was presented to college player Jeff Bentrim, quarterback for North Dakota State University, as the NCAA Division II Player of the Year.

When I had heard the whole story, Harlon became a hero to me, and I looked forward to the opportunity to meet him. One afternoon, I picked up the phone and made a nervous call to the only professional football player—other than Cornell Green, who had signed me to the free-agent contract—I had ever spoken to.

"Harlon, this is Robert Steele, a friend of Jerry's." I had no idea what to expect, but I figured the direct approach was the best. "I've just signed a free-agent contract with the Dallas Cowboys, and I have absolutely no clue what I'm about to get into. Jerry thought it would be a good idea if I gave you a call. Would you mind spending a couple of hours with me?"

"Absolutely, Robert, when would you like to get together?"
Harlon couldn't have been nicer, and it was a huge relief to hear
such a friendly voice.

"This week would be great, if it's not too much to ask. I'm
about to fly to Dallas on Friday, and I'd like to talk with you
before I go. Would Thursday work?"

"Thursday's a go. See you at the football field at ten."

Harlon and I met at the field, and instead of just sitting down
and starting to chat about the culture of the league—what the
locker room atmosphere was going to be, how guys would treat
the rookies, that sort of thing—we started out with some drills
and a few pass moves. Satisfied that I had an idea of what I was
doing on the field, Harlon sat me down and gave me the advice
I remember to this day:

- Get in great physical shape so you won't be mentally
  dragging when others are.

- Listen to your coaches.

- Watch what the other players are doing well.

- Pay attention to the small skills that make a difference.

- Run great routes. Let the quarterback know that he can
  rely on you to be where he expects you to be. Confidence
  is key. Trust between quarterbacks and receivers is a must.

In other words, work hard, and keep my eyes open and my
mouth shut. Good advice not matter what you're doing!

I was happy to listen to Harlon and saw in his eyes that he
was excited for me, which made me feel as though I had, in some
way, already entered the brotherhood of football professionals
who aspire to play at the highest level. He made me believe I
could accomplish what he had, and he encouraged me to stay
away from the negative influences always threatening to bring
down professional athletes. I didn't know exactly what he meant

until much later, but his voice, his demeanor, the NFL experience of more than a decade oozing from his pores—everything he said stuck with me, and I took it to heart.

His wisdom and honesty were refreshing as I listened to every word, knowing I would never hear the same thing from my own coaches. I didn't know the entire Harlon Hill story—especially what had happened toward the end of his career when he left Chicago for Pittsburgh and Detroit—nor did I press him for details. I sensed, though, that he either didn't play as long as he would have liked, or maybe he had allowed the same outside influences that he was warning me about to interrupt his career.

But the specific advice he did give me was priceless. Harlon was specific in explaining how not to stand out and call attention to myself for things people don't want to be noticed for:

- Speak only when spoken to.

- Listen twice as much as you speak.

- Don't be loud or rambunctious—and never try to be the life of the party.

- Focus on the everyday routine.

I spent many hours reflecting on that conversation during my time in Dallas and Thousand Oaks. For the first time, I understood the concept of becoming a full-speed "every day, every play" kind of player. I was I glad I had a chance to catch up with Harlon, Jerry, and the rest of the Hill family prior to completing *Steele Here* and told them how special Harlon was to me and how much he helped me prepare to play for the Cowboys.

Before my conversation with Harlon, I realized I had never gone full speed every day on every play, and I remembered working with Richard Smith four summers before, when playing professional football was the furthest thing from my mind. I was hearing the same message from two different people—both of whom spoke from experience, albeit much different ones and having reached much different levels of success.

Those new ideas were incubating in my fertile mind.

Going full speed every day on every play is what separates the great players from the average Joes, the guys who have a cup of coffee with a team, playing on the practice squad for a couple of seasons before going back home with a few good stories and a jersey. The phrase "perform in practice the way you want to perform in the game" began to take on new importance. Practice wasn't meant as punishment, as I'd always thought before. Practice improves players by placing them in game situations, mirroring game conditions as closely as possible. That attention to detail is what allows teams like the Dallas Cowboys to be "on" every weekend. Many players don't run as fast in practice as they do in a game, they take plays off, they look for shortcuts—and then they wonder why the quarterback's timing is off or why he's choosing other options on pass plays.

"Full speed, every day, every play" was going to be my new motto. I still live it today.

Harlon helped me shape a significant new mindset as I was preparing to go to Dallas for rookie orientation. I needed to get comfortable with all the people who would be in camp. I wanted to see what I would be up against. Would the players from the bigger schools like USC, UCLA, Texas, Oklahoma, or Ohio State intimidate me? I wasn't sure. I needed to see it all for myself. I needed to learn as many plays as I could by working with the quarterbacks and showing them I would catch every ball they threw my way.

Harlon taught me how to keep my head in the game. "Go forward, young man, I'm pulling for you," I remember Harlon saying as I pulled out of the parking lot after our meeting. "Learn to put up with the rookie crap. That's part of the game. Expect it. The more crap they give you, the more they like you, and the more they want you to make the team," he said with a smile. "It's a little like life, right? If they don't pay any attention to you, it's because they don't like you, and you'll be gone by Monday."

He patted the roof of the car, and I drove off.

I grew from that meeting. A new mindset was replacing my loose, fun college style. That new mindset was "whatever it takes, for as long as I could take it, without any complaints, pushing ahead, never looking up or around at any distractions that might detract my focus from my ultimate goal of making the team."

In other words, I was going to show up and shut up, exactly as Harlon had instructed.

Red Zone Rules

Go Mental

"Full speed, every day, on every play" becomes the underdog's motto when faced with insurmountable odds. That mental mantra focuses you on what you have to achieve and pushes you forward when you're physically and mentally tired. In our society, the underdog has to prove himself daily. Mental focus is a stepping-stone to success.

"You've got to have physical talent to perform well at any level—high school, college, or professional football. But you've not only got to have extraordinary physical talent, you've got to be mentally strong and committed and confident in what you do," says Roger Staubach.

No one knows more about mental toughness than Roger, a Heisman Trophy winner at the United States Naval Academy and a Hall of Fame performer from the time he stepped on the field for the Dallas Cowboys in 1969. No player's character was more highly thought of than Roger's (after graduating from the Naval Academy, he served a tour of duty in Vietnam before joining the Cowboys), and even today, players look to the two-time Super Bowl champ for guidance.

"As an athlete, you have to transfer that confidence to other people like your coaches and teammates. For me, hard work produced confidence, the knowledge that whatever I practiced would carry over to game situations. I was always confident because I knew I had paid the price to be ready for that moment.

"Mental strength—living in the *moment* and focusing on the *moment*—means you give the best that you can on every play. When you have mental strength, you're going to deliver the very best you have."

Follow the Bouncing Ball

For most players, practicing sports is drudgery. Players hate to practice, but they love to play in the games. What most people don't understand is something I heard Coach Landry say many times to the team: "Isn't it interesting that the better prepared team seems to have the ball bounce its way?"

In other words, Tom Landry didn't believe in luck. He believed that the better prepared teams created their own luck by taking advantage of superior preparation and recognizing opportunity.

The Cowboys, a perennial powerhouse, always seemed to have the ball bounce their way. Roger Staubach could direct a two-minute drive like nobody's business.

Why were the Cowboys that good?

Because Coach Landry believed in hard work, practicing plays at full speed, being in the right place at the right time. Call it luck if you want.

I call it Landry's Law: Proper Preparation Prevents Poor Performance and Prepares Pro Players to Practice Perfection.

Coach Landry saw the bounces of the ball not as random chance, but as opportunities to showcase our preparedness—and he never hesitated to put our preparedness up against that of any other team.

Tom Landry won 270 NFL games—including two Super Bowls, five NFC championships, and thirteen division titles—as Cowboys' head coach.

Coincidence?

I don't think so.

5

Dallas, Texas

Let's Get Physical

The rookies, some ninety-two of us, arrive for orientation. We'll be tested for speed, quickness, agility, and strength. We'll be checked-up and checked out.

It's time to show who we are and what we bring to camp.

Or we go home.

I landed in Dallas with competing emotions. Even though I knew I was ready to give the NFL a shot, I felt the same mix of excitement and dread that accompanied Cornell Green's call to me to announce that he'd be coming to Florence to talk about a free-agent contract. Excitement about what I would be experiencing over the course of the next few months. Dread for the unknown of how I would perform against these big-time college superstars. Just months in my past, that call seemed like a lifetime ago.

In some ways, I suppose, it was.

An exciting new season in my life had started, and the next two months of football training would determine my future. I kept Harlon's advice in mind: *You have nothing to brag about. You have everything to prove.*

I checked into my hotel and headed to the fourteenth floor for a team physical, proudly joining the ranks of my fellow hopefuls, who ranged in age from twenty-one to twenty-nine. We were paraded in our underwear from station to station while being poked and prodded. The long line included the other free agents—the long shots—as well as the Cowboys' twelve draft choices, led by Larry Bethea. At six foot five and 250 pounds—big for any player in the 1970s—the defensive lineman was the team's number one pick out of Michigan State.

The physical was going along nicely until the doctor looked at my knees and said, "You've had both cut, huh?"

Pretty obvious, I thought. Back in those days, doctors hadn't developed some of the neat-and-tidy techniques players have access to today, so the operations had left me with one hard-to-miss nine-inch zipper on my left knee and two smaller scars on my right. Dr. Jack Hughston, the renowned orthopedic surgeon from my hometown, had done amazing work on my two knees and forced me to rehab them to be stronger than they were prior to my injuries.

"Is there a problem?" I shot back. I hadn't even seen the practice field, and the doctor's line of questioning was making me think that I might not. "Those surgeries were more than two years ago. The Cowboys know about them. I've played two seasons since with absolutely no issues."

His next comment caught me off guard.

"Would you be willing to sign a waiver? That way, if you hurt your knees in camp, the Cowboys won't be responsible for paying you."

"Sure." I didn't hesitate. I knew my knees were strong enough to handle the strain, and I was faster now than even prior to the surgeries.

The doctor worked his way up my back. A moment later, another question: "How many times have you dislocated your shoulder?"

"None that I know about, but I've taken a few hits, for sure." In that instant, I thought about a handful of hits over my four-year college career that left me with stingers in my shoulders and neck, the kind of hits where white stars really do pop up in front of your eyes and your legs feel like wet noodles. One time, in particular, I had run to the wrong sideline after a defensive back had clotheslined me on a third down play. I stood there until one of the opposing players was gracious enough to remind me that I should be on the other side of the field.

I wondered whether any permanent damage had been done.

"Would you be willing to sign a waiver on both of your shoulders?" he asked.

Why am I not surprised?

"Absolutely," I told him confidently. "Where's the paperwork?"

"What about your neck? Would you sign a waiver for that?"

"Yes." The whole thing was getting a little ridiculous, and I sensed that the doctor was playing the moment for a good laugh. I wasn't laughing, though. I was signing away any right to compensation so that the Cowboys wouldn't have the least liability if I went out on the practice field and ended my career on the first snap.

It was a liberating experience, because I knew I would be able to go through with the camp workouts. It was also one of the most isolating experiences of my life, putting me out there alone on an ocean of uncertainty, where I would either sink or swim, and no one or nothing would be there to be buoy me up.

Before the doctor asked me to sign a waiver for the next body part, like my hands and my back, I couldn't resist making a joke: "Sir, we're on the fourteenth floor of this hotel. If you told me that by jumping off I would make the team, I would head for that exit right now." I nodded in the direction of a plate-glass window overlooking the city. The implication was clear. "Does that answer your question?"

"You're pretty serious about this, aren't you?" He acknowledged my conviction with a thin smile and a nod. That comment made me realize that he knew what rights I was signing away even though I really didn't know or really care at that moment.

"I've got nothing to lose," I reminded him. "I just don't think anything bad will happen to me. I'll sign every paper you've got."

In all, I signed six waivers, confident that I was in the best shape of my life.

If you're worried about getting hurt, you shouldn't be playing football. That thought kept me going the rest of the day.

By the following morning, I'd put the incident out of my mind. I was ready to play football.

Boot Camp, Big D Style

I was on my way. All I needed to do was impress the coaches the next morning so I would be invited to summer workouts in Dallas, as Drew Pearson had been before making his mark in the NFL. Drew was a guy I admired, and I was looking forward to meeting him, but I also knew I'd be competing against him when the time came for us to go head-to-head in training camp. That was one of the things I had to realize early on. We were all there to take the job of someone who was on the team that won Super Bowl XII.

We went to the practice field, and the coaches put us through our speed trials: the 40-yard dash, a lot of 20-yard dashes, and the 10-yard dash. The last sprint, in particular, might seem like a pointless exercise—after all, how can one player be that much faster than another over a distance of thirty feet, which is about like running from the end of a room to the other—but the coaches were obsessed with speed coming off the ball.

In a league where every player has honed his game as close to perfection as possible, even a couple of inches makes all the difference.

That day, I ran as well as I did for Yaworski back at UNA—4.6 in the forty—but because of the conditioning I had done to prepare for the drills, I was faster off the ball than I had ever been. It didn't take me long to get to full stride, even with my long legs. I still didn't have great distance speed, but one of the coaches explained to me that they valued a good burst of speed over sustained speed, because even the best quarterbacks couldn't throw a ball the length of the field. All of them, though, were deadly accurate at 5, 10, and 20 yards.

The coaches were impressed more with my explosiveness and the fact that I was equal to some of the other—faster—guys for the shorter distances, which meant that I could get to the proper position in my routes so the quarterback—Roger Staubach, in this case—could hit me in stride.

I also did well in the rest of the trials—a 1.5 mile run and pass-pattern drills. There were also fifteen different tests for strength. Overall, I showed extremely well, running fast, jumping high with quick agility, and passing every other test the coaches threw my way.

One of the scouts even came up to me at the end of the day and gave me some encouragement. I felt as though I had passed my first test.

He asked me if I had any questions.

"Only one," I said. "Who offers invitations for the summer workouts in Dallas? Is that Coach Landry or someone else? Whoever it is, I'd like to speak with him." I knew even as I asked the question that it sounded presumptuous coming out of the mouth of a guy who was lucky to have gotten a plane ticket to

Dallas in the first place. Now I was asking to chat with Coach Landry to gauge my chances of making the team.

"You know, I want to prove that I'm worthy of an invitation to be here during the summer," I continued, when the scout just stood there dumbfounded. "I know that if I don't come here this summer, I won't make the team. I'm just putting it out there. If I've shown any hope or promise, I need to be one of those dozen players that you invite to camp, or I won't make the team."

"Only a few get that opportunity, but I'll put your name down," the scout told me, warming to the idea that I would be direct enough to ask such a question. "The invitations are a direct result of how well you performed today."

Put my name down isn't what I'm looking for. I pressed him further.

"Before I leave here, I'd like to speak to someone about my chances for coming to Dallas," I continued. I've never been shy when I needed to ask a question or find out what I needed to know or do to succeed. My dad always misquoted the Bible by saying, "You have not 'cause you ask not." Even though he mangled the words, the lesson never got old. That statement will get you more opportunities than you can handle, and my father was living proof of that. He taught me many things along the way. My sales career and my success as a salesman is a tribute to my father.

"Gil Brandt and Coach Landry make those decisions. Check with them at dinner tonight. But you didn't hear that from me, right?"

I thanked him and told him his secret was safe with me.

The evening meal at the hotel was a typical simple affair with meat, potatoes, salad, and dessert. I could barely eat as I nervously waited for the meal to conclude and for most of the other rookies to file out toward the bar, which had a disco. Dancing wasn't on my mind. Gil Brandt and Coach Landry were.

When dinner was over, I saw Gil preparing to leave. I walked quickly over to his table and threw my hand out. "Mr. Brandt. Robert Steele. It's a pleasure to meet you, sir."

"I know who you are," Gil shot back. He stood there and looked at me, and I thought for an instant that what I said next might make the difference between having a shot at making the team and spending the rest of my life back in Alabama regretting that I had never followed through.

"I wanted to find out what it will take for me to be invited to Dallas to work out this summer. I know from the materials you sent me a couple of months ago that that's how Drew Pearson made the team. . . ."

"It takes an invitation from Coach Landry," Gil said, softening a bit. I could tell he'd had this conversation before, and he still hadn't forgotten what it was like to be a young man with a dream and the desire to make it happen. "I've not seen all of the results from today's drills, but I've heard some good feedback. We'll be in touch." He patted me on the shoulder and turned toward a coach who had come up to talk to him. I knew that pat was my invitation to leave.

I was encouraged by what Gil said about my performance in the drills—at least he had some idea of who I was—but thought, *There they go again, telling me they will be in touch. This is beginning to sound like a broken record.*

I wasn't sure how I compared with the rest of the hopefuls, but I started to do the math in my head: the twelve draft choices would be invited, and they all may or may not show up. That would leave a couple of spots for guys like me—the underdogs. So why not get my name out there and see what would come of it? The worst they could tell me was no.

Still, I was surprised when the phone rang three days later. A call from Dallas.

"Robert, your insistence on coming to Dallas was heard."

I don't remember asking the name of the caller, and all these years later, I have no idea who was on the other end of the line pronouncing my future with the Cowboys.

"You showed extremely well in rookie orientation," the voice continued. "Honestly, you did better than we thought you would. You're in pretty good shape, and you've got desire. We want to bring you to Dallas."

I must have sat there for a few seconds without saying anything. I was stunned.

"We have only one issue," the man said. I could hear a hint of a smile in his voice. I'm sure I wasn't the first player to be struck dumb by a call like that. "We will not pay you any money until training camp officially opens. We will provide you with an apartment with three other guys, but your meal expenses won't be covered."

No problem. Beanie Weenies isn't a bad diet. My favorite is a good peanut butter and jelly sandwich. I can eat those every day if I have to.

My invitation came! That was what mattered.

"If you can supply me with an apartment," I said, trying to keep a quaver out of my voice from the excitement I felt. "I don't need anything more. I'm in!" My payment would be a free apartment for working like a dog. But I was on my way, my intermediate goal accomplished.

Now, I thought, *focus on the big goal.*

Five days later, I packed my Trans Am, a car my parents had given me as a college graduation present, and headed to Dallas. I was the first in my family to make it past freshman year in college, let alone graduate. Given the fact that my college tuition was free, I think my parents felt sorry for me and bought me the car.

Leaving Columbus, Georgia, in the rearview mirror brought tears to my eyes, just as it had four years earlier when I left for college. I would miss the place, but I would also embrace the greatest journey of my life. I was off to a new city and new experiences, thrown together with people I didn't know—all at age twenty-one. An interesting contrast, tears in my eyes, excitement in my heart and a belief that I was about to change my life forever.

This was my first road trip, more than a state away from Georgia and I wasn't sure what to expect.

Big Times in Big D

I was on edge for the entire fourteen-hour trip, with a thousand thoughts racing through my mind.

Do I have enough money to last me the summer?

Who's going to help me when I get there?

What will my workout schedule be like?

Could this be the trip that makes me a Dallas Cowboy?

I mentally rehearsed my summer plan constantly, to the point that I was obsessed with every detail. From the moment I woke up in the morning, to the time I dropped my head on the pillow at night, I had but one thought. I would work out every day, as many hours as the practice facility would be open, to be in the best possible shape when it came time to report to camp. Harlon had told me what to do. I just now had to execute on what he had told me that hot sultry morning at Brooks High School outside of Florence, Alabama.

I wasn't being paid for this, but I had my $2,500 signing bonus. Not a lot of money, but probably enough. A gallon of gas was $0.60, a dozen eggs a little less than that, and it's not like I was going to be spending a lot of time sampling the Dallas nightlife. With luck, that bonus would last me through the summer.

While I wasn't really concerned about money, I was apprehensive that the little details might distract me from my goal. It was the first time I had ever truly feared the unknown.

But my gut told me, *You'll make it. See it, believe it, achieve it.* My positive mental image of making the team kept me going every day. I knew I could never relax, never let my guard down. I couldn't quit. I would do anything and everything the coaches asked. My will and my intention were strong and would be assets to me in the coming days.

Almost in Dallas, I felt excitement rise as I hit the final stretch. Like Drew Pearson, I had been asked to come to Dallas early. I believed because of that invitation I had a chance at making the team. The Trans Am—identical to the one made famous in the Burt Reynolds and Jerry Reed movie *Smokey and the Bandit* except it was brown with an eagle on the front hood—roared on. I was traveling on Interstate 20 at eighty-five miles an hour when I looked over and saw a state trooper giving me the evil eye.

He didn't turn around, and I never looked back. I took that as a good sign as I raced on toward Dallas, the wind at my back and the pedal to the floor.

I arrived a few hours later to a stifling Dallas summer. Far from being put off by the heat and humidity, I embraced it. After all, it wasn't much different from what I was accustomed to in Columbus, Georgia. Columbus is on the Chattahoochee River—a Native American name meaning "river of painted rock"—nestled in a valley in west-central Georgia, just across the river from Phenix City, Alabama. Every summer is like a sauna, and you either make peace with that fact early in your life, or you move to a more suitable climate. May through September is hot, sweaty, and unbearable, no two ways about it. Since summer had always been my favorite time of the year, though, I couldn't wait to get started. I knew I could handle the heat and humidity. Maybe the boys from northern schools might not.

I arrived at the workout facility on Forest Lane, just east of town. Buck Buchanan, the longtime equipment manager, handed me a key and gave me directions to the apartment. After the anticipation I felt while driving to Dallas, my arrival was nothing special—no welcoming committee, no hundred-piece brass band, no Cowboys cheerleaders.

In fact, few guys had even shown up yet. Maybe that wasn't the worst news I could have had. The quiet gave me a chance to get my bearings and to remember why I was there in the first place.

The next day, a few more rookies arrived, including two from small colleges, guys who became my workout buddies. Dave Kraayeveld had played at tiny Milton College in Wisconsin and Rod Bockwaldt at Weber State in Utah. Dave and I were the most regular in our workout schedules, and Rod occasionally slept in a bit and came to the weight room later in the morning. In fact, I'd say Dave and I were downright religious in our daily devotion to working out, spending from 8:30 a.m. until 5:30 p.m. every day of the week getting in prime condition for the most important challenges of our lives. I would have worked out longer, but the training facility was open only for those hours, probably to keep guys from burning themselves out before we got to training camp.

I didn't waste the weekends, either, because Saturday and Sunday were perfect days for running. I would run five to seven miles on those days so I wouldn't lose any stamina prior to starting the process all over again on Monday morning. On Saturday afternoon, I might find a basketball game or take a stroll by the swimming pool at Southern Methodist University. Among the few joys I had that summer were the Saturday afternoons when I hung out at the SMU pool and met "normal" people, including a few of the attractive SMU lifeguards. What a breath of fresh air to find a few non-football people to spend time with.

People tend to laugh when I tell them what we did for entertainment during that summer—and it had nothing to do with strip clubs and exotic dancers. That may be how the veterans entertained themselves, but the rookies didn't have any money, nor were we in any shape after our long days to do anything but fall into the pool every evening before crawling out and going straight to bed. The most exciting event was when one of the rookies found a tarantula in his room, and he brought the spider to my apartment and microwaved it. Probably something PETA might not agree with, but those guys had a good time with the creature.

Then there was the time my car was floured as a parting gift, as I was headed back to Columbus to see my parents prior to training camp. The thought of leaving my car in an unfamiliar city I might not see again didn't appeal to me. At the end of our time together, when the rookies were checking out of the apartments on July 10, someone poured white flour all over my brown car. Fortunately, I had put the T-tops on from our ride the night before. Later, I found out that the person who committed the dastardly deed was Harold Randolph, an eighth-round draft pick who was cut halfway through camp.

On the few nights when we weren't just completely exhausted, Dave, Rod, and I would take the T-tops off my Trans-Am and take in the bright lights of the big city. Almost every conversation with my new friends ended the same way it had started: *What will making the team be like?* I always kept my opinions to myself, because I didn't like to get the cart ahead of the horse, as my dad might say. Still, my mantra that summer was *I WILL make this team.* I never left any room for doubt, and I never shared my conviction with my new best friends. I knew they would see my statement as total arrogance.

Always, no matter what we were doing, I had Harlon's good advice ringing in my ears: *Keep your head down and your mouth shut. Show what you can do on the field because coaches don't want to hear about what you do off the field. They only want to see what you can do on the field.*

I didn't stop long enough to catch my breath because I knew that every moment before the July 15 start date was a precious one. I worked out, lifted weights, ran pass patterns—and then lifted more weights. The practice facility had both racquetball and basketball courts, and I took advantage of those when I wasn't doing something else. Then I would run more pass patterns for Glen Carano, Danny White, and occasionally even Roger Staubach. Whenever a quarterback showed up to work on their timing, I volunteered to run pass patterns until I couldn't take another step.

There was a method to my madness. When it came time to join training camp, the quarterbacks would all be more comfortable with me because of the hundreds of pass patterns we had run together during the summer.

Rod, Dave, and I were the Three Musketeers that summer, standing in solidarity to our goal: *Whatever it takes, we're going to do it*, we had promised one another. We talked a lot about our common dream of making the team, wondering what our chances were, imagining what training camp might be like. We pushed each other, but because we played different positions, we were never in competition, which helped push all three of us to reach toward our common goal.

None of the other rookie free agents worked out with the same vigor. Kraayeveld was a defensive lineman, so while I ran pass patterns, he lifted weights. Repetition on those pass patterns was what got me in such tremendous shape and enabled me to run like a deer. I had never felt so good in my life—like my legs were springs and my heart and lungs a perfectly oiled machine—and after a point, I never got tired.

The state-of-the-art workout facilities and a total lack of

outside influences (including those college friends I would have loved to have seen but am glad I didn't, as they would have been huge distractions) created a perfect setting to get in shape and to come to a much better understanding of the effort, energy, and dedication required to make the team. Our only escape every day was the Pizza Hut and its all-you-can-eat buffet next door to the training center. For less than five dollars, we ate enough to fill us up so we wouldn't be hungry at night and spend extra money on food. The only problem with the all-you-can-eat buffet was that many of the guys returned to the apartment for an afternoon nap. Not me, though, because in the afternoons, the quarterbacks might show up.

I was always around the facility and had gotten something of a reputation as a gym rat. Watching the veterans come and go and occasionally having them acknowledge me or speak to me was always a treat. Studying how Billy Joe Dupree, Robert Newhouse, Charlie Waters, Cliff Harris, Roger Staubach, Randy Hughes, and others worked out gave me an excellent opportunity to interact with the guys who had already made their mark on the game.

Six weeks later after arriving in Dallas with nothing but a dream—and after running countless miles, thousands of pass patterns, and lifting tons and tons of weight—I was ready to take on the world.

Red Zone Rules

Be a Gladiator

See it, believe it, achieve it.

"Perseverance is crucial. You've got to have thick skin. You're trained to have confidence from the first day you strap on the pads," says Charlie Waters, who played twelve stellar seasons for the Cowboys at defensive back and quickly became one of the most feared hitters in the league. A converted quarterback and wide receiver, Charlie was a versatile athlete who knew that, given any opportunity, he could get the job done.

"You've got to be able to pound your chest and be bigger and stronger than the other person, because they're out to get you. Out on that field, it's kill or be killed."

Getting Knocked to Your Knees— and Coming Back

Positive mental images focus your mind on your goal like tunnel vision. The only voice in your head is the inner coach who tells you to keep going and never quit. If you really want to achieve your goals, your will must be strong enough to override any distraction. You'll grab the brass ring, because you will have earned it.

The prize for your effort: the feeling of competent confidence, which is more than feeling good and having esteem. Competence implies that you're rock-solid in your skills. Confidence means that you have a healthy and positive regard for what is needed. Confidence means that you know, more than believe, that you will achieve.

"My first impression of Robert was that he was a tall wide receiver who wanted to do everything," says Gil Brandt. "He wanted to be on the kickoff team, on the punting team. He would catch the ball coming across the middle, something that even veterans don't very often want to do. What I remember about him most, though, was his personality. He always made me believe that he'd never had a bad day in his life. He was one of those upbeat guys who you loved to be around and have on your team. He was always positive. Robert came to me and told me about his car being floured at the apartment. Robert did not want to give me the name of the person who committed the deed. I pressed him and told him it would not affect his status but I needed to know. He finally told me, and I knew Robert felt bad about his car but worse about having to tell me what happened."

Leave it to the great Vince Lombardi to put it even more succinctly: "The real glory is being knocked to your knees and then coming back. That's real glory."

Flypaper

"I was a defensive player, so we were always going against the offense in practices. I often watched Robert catching the football. He had incredible hands. I started calling him 'Flypaper,' because the ball would just stick to him," says Bruce Huther.

"Some of my buddies on defense also picked up the term. We all started calling him Flypaper from there on. He would just make these phenomenal catches. His talent caught everybody's eye. There were times when you'd hear people go '*wow!*' Just one great catch after another. So, that's what stood out about Robert, something I'll always remember about him. He would have a defensive back all over him and he was making these leaping catches, the kind where you'd say, 'No way.' And the ball would just stick to his hands."

6

Training Camp

Staubach's Pound Cake

My grandmother, Gladys Kerlin, was a good-hearted soul who never knew a stranger. She also knew absolutely nothing about football. But when she read the materials that the Cowboys had sent me in the run-up to camp, she grew particularly interested in "this Roger Staubach character." She had heard me tell stories about him—at that point (heck, and even today), he was as much of an idol as any player in the NFL—and Gladys decided that if I thought so highly of him, then so did she.

Before I headed to camp, my grandmother made one of her world-famous pound cakes and asked me to give it to Roger Staubach when I got to California. Her specific instructions were, "Now make sure that when you get to camp, you give half of this to Roger, because it will mean something to him." She gave me a sly wink. "And it will be a good thing for you, too."

I've never been so embarrassed in my life. She carefully placed it in a box specially designed for pound cake and tied it up with a piece of bailing twine. Here I was headed to an NFL camp—a warrior preparing to do battle with the best football players on the planet—and I was carrying a pound cake, of all things. As embarrassed as I was, no one crossed Gladys.

Besides, I'd been around her enough to know that she was always right.

When I arrived at camp, I let the pound cake sit in my room until the quarterbacks arrived three days later. Three days after that, I knew I had to do something.

This is really cheesy. I don't want to do this. That's what I heard from the devil that sits on one shoulder; the angel on my other shoulder was telling me to do the right thing.

But it got to the point where I couldn't glare at the cake any longer, couldn't hear anything but my sweet grandmother's parting words to me. I sure couldn't face her later that summer and tell her that I hadn't given Roger the cake. She might have understood, but she would have been disappointed.

So that afternoon, I sliced that pound cake in half and carried it to Roger.

"Roger, I know you don't know my grandmother, and I'm sure you'll probably never meet her. But she wanted me to deliver this," I put the cake down in front of him. He was still a little shell-shocked from the way I had just barged in to his Cal Lutheran dorm room and started this eccentric story about a cake and my grandmother and her plan for ingratiating me to a Hall of Fame quarterback who might hold my fate in his hands.

"Anyway, half of this pound cake is for you."

Instead of dismissing me—which he certainly would have been well within his rights to do—he responded in a way for which I'll always be grateful.

"Pound cake's my favorite," he said with a big, honest smile on his face. "Camp sure isn't the place to get something this good."

He walked over to the kitchenette and got a fork and chipped a hunk off his half.

"This hits the spot," he said, grabbing a couple more bites. "Thanks, rookie."

I knew my grandmother was right. You make friends by being friendly. No matter whom you encounter, being friendly wins people to your side almost every time.

When word got around that there was some real food in the area, several guys were looking at Roger, wanting a piece of his cake. Roger said, "Steele's grandmother wanted me to have this to sustain me through camp. This is for me. You guys get out of here."

Everybody laughed and walked out. It was one memorable moment of a remarkable summer.

Thousand Oaks, California

July 15 heralded opening day of the Cowboys Training Camp for rookies and veterans. Rookies arrived first. Ten days later, the veterans rolled in. What a contrast in styles. The rookies, to a man, were nervous, tight, and had their heads on swivels—who really knew what to expect? The veterans who reported early, on the other hand, seemed to have everything under control.

In hindsight, I understand that what separated the rookies from the veterans wasn't so much talent, but a working knowledge of the process. Even guys who had gone through it once had a huge advantage over those of us who stared in wide-eyed wonder at everything going on around us.

Every year, the Cowboys hosted the six-week camp in Thousand Oaks, California, at Cal Lutheran College, just north of Los Angeles, where the team had been training for several years. The venue made sense. The veterans didn't face the distractions they would have at home in Dallas, and the rookies would have felt out of place no matter where the camp had been situated.

While the rookies were members of the Dallas Cowboys organization, we weren't officially part of the team until that dreaded final cut on September 1, after the last preseason game. Although the veterans weren't outwardly nervous, many of them who felt certain they would make the team had no guaranteed spots in Tom Landry's house. Injuries, an untimely fall from grace, a hotshot rookie—in the NFL, so many things can happen to derail a career that no one really feels secure. The thought that we all kept pushing to the back of our minds was that every day, every play could be the last, because the Cowboys were always top-grading their talent and sloughing off the players who clearly couldn't help the team to reach another Super Bowl.

The team routinely brought in more than fifty free agents every year (some years that number might top one hundred). The veterans knew the Cowboys would keep only three or four free agents and draft picks every year—the draft choices were always the surest bets of making the team—but seeing all those hungry free agents at the very least kept the veterans honest, even if they had won the Super Bowl just a few months before camp opened. Free agents knew their road was tough, but the Cowboys team was one of the few that gave free agents a shot at making it. You took what you could get.

History proved that miracles could happen, with players like Dan Reeves, Cornell Green, Cliff Harris, and Drew Pearson having made the team against all odds. For every one of those guys, though, there were hundreds of players around the country who went to camp and came away with a few good stories they could tell their buddies at the bar and the memory of having become—*almost*—a Dallas Cowboy. This summer wouldn't be any different.

Training camp was a place for separation.

The Cowboys separated you from your friends and family for those six weeks, and they also separated you from the reality of everyday life in Dallas and from the veterans, both on the practice field—through different colored pants—and in the dining hall.

The separation was purposeful, and the coaches made a point of contact and conversation that established, without any doubt, the organization's hierarchy and ensured that the rookies were kept in their place.

The on-field crush certainly wasn't any easier than the mental hurdles we had to get over. That first week rookies had two full-contact practices a day in full pads, a grueling schedule that brought even players who had survived four years at major Division I colleges to their knees. A lot of college players think they're ready for anything until they suit up against the veterans. Very few of them feel that way after fifteen minutes into the first practice.

Training camp was a pressure cooker in every sense of the word. The psychological pressure was so intense because every player's contract has a clause stipulating performance: if you're not playing up to NFL standards, the organization can release you from your contract, no questions asked. The coaches for every team in the NFL define their standards, and the Cowboys' standards were the highest in the league.

Having studied contract law in college, I reviewed my contract during training camp and looked back at all those waivers I had agreed to in the heat of the moment. Part of me wished I had taken my time to consider what I was signing away, but I knew that no matter how long I had put the doctor off when he put the papers in front of me, my decision would have been the same. Now that I was in camp, I knew the risks were plenty. If I got hurt, the Cowboys owed me nothing. Shortly after camp began, I realized that I was going down a one-way street the wrong way—and I couldn't have cared less.

Aside from trying to live up to the Cowboys' impossibly high standards, the media onslaught added another layer of distraction.

Since the Cowboys were the reigning champs, journalists followed us everywhere—even the rookies, most of whom would be on the chopping block in the first couple of weeks and would never be heard from again. The press were most interested in following the rookie draft choices, especially Larry Bethea and Todd Christianson, the team's top two picks and those likely to make the biggest splash (or the biggest flop, which would have been at least as interesting a read in the morning papers) at the beginning of the season.

Larry was given a $100,000 signing bonus, paltry in comparison with some of today's contracts (University of Georgia quarterback Matthew Stafford was chosen first by the Detroit Lions in the 2009 NFL draft and signed a contract that guaranteed him $41.7 million). My $2,500 signing bonus seemed large to me, but insignificant to the rest of the Cowboys. The signing bonus didn't necessarily mean that Larry would make the team—especially if he performed poorly in camp—but the Cowboys' scouting system wouldn't look good if Larry didn't pan out. For that reason, he was virtually assured a spot, while people like me with a less impressive pedigree fought every day just to get noticed.

To say that the Dallas Cowboys training camp was dog-eat-dog would be like saying Beethoven wrote some good songs.

Veterans watched the rookie cuts closely and breathed a sigh of relief when the new guys started dropping like flies. The vets knew the rookies were there for their jobs, and the longer the rookies hung around, the better their shot at upsetting one of the vets for a roster spot. In today's terms, a player wanted to be the American Idol of the Dallas Cowboys. Tom Landry, though, was a much harsher judge of talent than Simon Cowell could ever be.

The Depth Chart

When I arrived, I looked at the depth chart posted at the facility and didn't know if I should laugh or cry. I was listed sixteenth out of sixteen on the depth chart for rookie receivers. Of course, the list didn't include the four returning veterans, Drew Pearson, Golden Richards, Butch Johnson, and Tony Hill—all of whom had made their bones in the organization and were going to be sporting Super Bowl rings at the start of the season. So, technically, I was the last man on a twenty-man roster of receivers. Suffice to say that my odds of making the team were, well, not great. I did see one positive aspect of being number twenty, though—I had nowhere to go but up.

Demoting me was not an option. Cutting me was.

Traditionally, the Cowboys carried only four wide receivers, so the odds of any of the sixteen of us who worked out behind the veterans making the roster were slim to none and—as my buddy Dave Kraayeveld was fond of saying—slim was last seen on a Greyhound bus headed toward New Orleans.

Job one for me became that of a silent self-promoter, and I set as my goal to do something every day to be noticed on the field. If coaches didn't notice me on a given day, I could very well be gone the next day without a trace. I remember wondering on more than one occasion what had happened to the guy who stood next to me the day before in calisthenics. I wondered if he had ever really been there. It was like the memory hole in George Orwell's *1984*, where reality could change without anyone's knowledge. That thought forced me to move through every drill with a precision that never seemed all that important in college. If a quarterback threw a pass my way or I had a chance to block someone, the play had to be spectacular.

In most cases, the Cowboys didn't cut players because they lacked physical ability, but for an inability to focus. The game took enough effort without the players giving in to distractions.

Making a physical error—falling down on a route, over-pursuing on a tackle or a block, even the occasional penalty—could be excused. Forgetting your assignment on a play was unforgivable. Coaches would fight for players they knew would survive mentally. But once a coach lost confidence in your mental ability, the same coaches would be quicker to ignore a player who looked to them for validation.

Nobody who ever went to an NFL training camp forgot that professional football was a business, and the job of the coaches was to put the best possible product on the field. That didn't leave any room for emotion to enter into the equation.

For example, I learned my assignments from the Cowboys rookie playbook in three days. Just when I had gotten to the point where I began to recite plays in my sleep, the coaches would shift to new plays they had inserted the night before. The game was mental and physical, shifting and changing, and I danced with it. The edge I had was that I never tired physically—the time I spent working out in Dallas was invaluable—and could hold my focus as long as anybody on the team, including the vets. Players who lose their physical edge also fatigue mentally, and early in the camp, it became easy to tell who those guys were going to be.

I spent the summer proving my work ethic and displaying my desire to make the team to the coaches and my fellow team members. Later, I realized that my loyalty to my teammates wasn't nearly as important to them as it was to me—in truth, I was the only one who wanted me to make it—and while football is a team sport, training camp is the loneliest place on earth for those six weeks.

You truly are separated from reality. You're alone. No one is pulling for you. And the odds are stacked against you. That time in Dallas wasn't just important to my success, it made me. I would never have had the same regime at home and I knew it. No way!

Yet those who could survive that mental challenge could physically handle anything thrown their way. What mattered to me was my mental focus, my strength from being in top shape, and my inner strength. It mattered to me because I was in such good physical shape that I never got winded throughout camp. Not even for a moment. I focused on the job, never feeling any of the pain the other rookies experienced. Strange as that may seem, running and running and running some more did not bother me. I welcomed it and watched as others tired and complained, and I am sure they thought I was either mental or on some kind of special sauce cooked only to my liking. I was. It was called focus.

The pay for training camp was $420 per week. Seven days a week, fifteen hours a day, that translates to about four dollars an hour. I could have made better money waiting tables at the restaurant a couple of blocks from the workout facility. Of course, my being in training camp with the Cowboys didn't have anything to do with money.

No, it was all about the payoff.

So Much to Prove, So Little Time

Life is good for a veteran; not so much for a rookie. The first ten days of rookie camp were intense. We got to know each other a little bit and started to settle in to a routine. Then the veterans showed up in their white pants on the afternoon of July 25. The white pants were a team tradition reserved for veterans, signaling to the rookies the real beginning of camp—and the beginning of the winnowing process that would trim nearly every player around me from the roster.

We've arrived, rookies. Watch out. We know you've been here for a while already, but this is our field. And we're wearing the white pants!

I remember the feeling that afternoon when the veterans strutted in to practice. It was like the gladiators had arrived, and we were lambs to the slaughter. These veterans were the real deal, and their aura—all intensity and intimidation—was like a noose around a rookie's neck, drawing tighter with every great catch, bone-jarring hit, or pancake block. Many of the rookies were done the day the veterans arrived, never the same after watching the veterans take the field and declare war against anyone trying to take their spot on the roster. You could see it in the rookies' eyes. You could see it in their actions. Sometimes, a guy would wake up the morning after a particularly hard practice and just leave camp without any instigation, his way of being able to say years later, "I left on my terms."

When the rookie hazing began, as it does in all NFL camps, the veterans didn't pick on me—except to ask me once to sing a song. I obliged. I wasn't about to let them get the best of me, and I had Harlon Hill's words about blending in fresh in my mind. I wanted to bring attention to myself with my ability to play football, not sing. I was accepted as a rookie because I blended in—and spent a lot of time both on and off the field showing my true colors.

I look back on my six weeks in Dallas as the great equalizer. I knew a lot of the veterans. I watched each of them work out every day. I'd had brief conversations with many of them. Sure, they kept their distance from me as their way of protecting themselves—and me—by not getting too close to any player in camp.

The separation occurred in every way. Rookies wore twenty-year-old game pants. Veterans wore nice, new white practice pants. Seeing the difference for the first time was an emotional jolt. The rookies had become comfortable with each other in practice scrimmages during the first two weeks. Now, every practice focused on the veterans.

After the first couple of weeks, even with twice-weekly cuts, I was still tenth on the depth chart for rookies. But I had moved up and watched and learned as others moved out. Now, ten of us were pitted against the four veterans, Drew, Tony, Butch, and Golden, for practice time and passes thrown our way. My rep time went down to almost nothing after the veterans reported. Rookies were in a real catch-22 when it came to getting noticed: it's awfully hard to catch a coach's attention when you're not getting the ball; only the veterans were getting full reps and running pass routes with Roger Staubach and Danny White, the two quarterbacks who would be instrumental in the team's push to repeat as Super Bowl champs. The rookies were relegated to Glen Carano and the five rookie QBs in camp.

The noose squeezed tighter and tighter. Any mistake toward the end of training camp becomes magnified, and I saw more than one player who, after making a bonehead play on the field or turning the ball over or missing a tackle, sit on the bench with his head in his hands, fully understanding that his football career—his passion and his love for the last decade of his life—had suddenly come to an end.

There were two locker rooms. The veterans had a separate locker room, the varsity facility at Cal Lutheran, while the rookies were stuck in a PE cubby half the size for twice as many people. Two rookies shared a small locker. Dave Kraayeveld, Rod Bockwaldt, Brian Billick, Todd Christenson, Dennis Thurman, and the remaining rookies didn't mind the inconvenience. We were all treated the same, with the exception of Larry Bethea. While Bethea lockered with us, we knew he wanted to be in the veteran locker room.

Could we blame him? Nope. He knew he would make the team. For him, it was only a matter of time before he would be wearing the white pants, and he knew it. The rookie antics seemed a waste of his time. Every other guy in the PE locker room fought for his life every day, while Bethea sauntered around as if he were a veteran already.

Conditions were cramped, but every day things got less and less crowded as rookies cleared out their lockers and headed home. Actually, the locker room became quite comfortable toward the end of camp, because there seemed to be fewer and fewer of us each day. Once that started happening, those of us who still survived wondered what it was like to meet with Landry for the final time.

None of us looked forward to that experience and put it out of our minds the best we could. In fact, the locker-room talk was often more like therapy than what you would expect from a bunch of testosterone-fueled young men trying to win a position on an NFL team. Talk generally came around to how we would handle the conversation with Coach Landry if—or, more likely, when—it ever came time to see him and what we would do when we headed back to "real life."

What struck me most was that so many of these phenomenal guys—players from the biggest schools in the country, great athletes who had been groomed from childhood to perform on the football field—were gone. Rookie raucous lowered its volume to a whisper as everybody began to understand that today could be his last.

Everything about training camp was Darwinian. Injuries played a big part of camp life. An injured veteran would give a rookie time to get some reps and to get his face in front of the coaches—not a good deal for the vets. And rookies who got hurt got sent home the moment they were back on the field. You could just about guarantee that a missed practice due to injury was the beginning of the end.

At the time, none of us saw this for what it really was: a cold financial decision. Those players who didn't sign the waivers—as I had—could, under the terms of their contract, get paid, even if they didn't make the team due to injury. But the Cowboys were well within their rights to cut a player immediately after he had come back from injury, a move that would trim the team's financial liability and stall one more rookie's dream.

Was I being kept around because of the waivers? The thought had entered my mind. But I didn't know, and I didn't care.

Camp was so intense that the veterans generally allowed a few rookies to get some reps in order to save their own legs for later. Those small moments could become important as camp continued. It was a good news/bad news situation: the reps always gave a rookie an opportunity to shine; substitute for a veteran and make a mistake, though, and you understood just how closely scrutinized your every move was, from the time you woke up until you went to bed.

So you want to be an NFL player, huh?

We came to fear the words, "Coach Landry would like to see you. Bring your playbook." We'd all heard about the Turk, the guy who ruined dreams when he tapped a rookie on the foot, waking him out of a dead sleep at 6 a.m. The timing wasn't random. Coaches sent the Turk before anybody was out of bed so the player could sneak out of camp without embarrassment.

Of course, nobody slept on Saturday or Tuesday nights because they knew the Turk—we had a nervous laugh one time when a fellow rookie said it was like waiting for the Candyman to show up to steal our souls—was coming to tap some feet. If you felt the tap, you knew what was coming next: "Coach Landry would like to see you. Bring your playbook." That meant you were going home, and your life as a Dallas Cowboy had officially ended.

The walk to Landry's office was a brief three minutes. The consequences lasted a lifetime. And out of seventy-nine other free agents invited to camp, one or two would be lucky enough to avoid meeting the Turk.

Red Zone Rules

Ski the Black Diamonds

"Being in an NFL training camp is highly competitive. You need both the physical strength and mental ability," says Gil Brandt, who, along with Tom Landry, masterminded the Cowboys' rise to greatness. Brandt, a football genius with an impeccable eye for talent, was the team's vice president for player personnel from 1960 to 1988.

"Every guy who comes to camp is already smart. When you talk about getting into football, you have to learn a foreign terminology, and you're expected to absorb a lot of information in a short period of time. We made it a point to bring our rookies in ahead of our veterans. It wouldn't have made any sense to have the rookies running around having no idea what 'red right formation' was or how to pull off a wham block.

"So the rookies are there for ten days, with a limited playbook, and then the veterans arrive. I can compare it to the same learning curve a skier has. Being a rookie is like standing at the top of the bunny slope and wondering how you're going to get down. When the veterans arrive, only ten days later, all of a sudden you're eyeing down a double black-diamond mogul field. Talk about fight-or-flight. The rookies see these stars—guys they've read and heard about, maybe even idolized or traded their football card or had their poster tacked to the wall of their bedroom—and can't believe how big and fast they are. The rookies are in awe of them, because most of them never thought they'd get to this place.

"Welcome the challenge. Learn to ski the black diamonds. Expect to perform at your peak."

Charles Darwin Was Right

"I was a free agent along with Robert, and I knew exactly what he was going through," says Bruce Huther, who played linebacker for the Cowboys from 1977 to 1980.

"But in either case, the guys you're competing against don't really want you to make that team. Sure, you pull for each other. But these are the guys you're competing against for your livelihood. Deep down, you want to grab the edge. You want to succeed, which means others have to fail.

"Even the coaches, at that point, don't want to spend much time with you until preseason gets going and they have a feel whether you're going to make it. Most of the guys who show up for those first few weeks are dead men walking as far as their football careers go. That's when you're on your own. Most players fail in the mental game three or four weeks in, just get overwhelmed by the grind.

"You wake up on a given morning, and somebody you've come to know is gone. That uncertainty keeps rookies on a constant edge, because they know going in how terrible the odds are that any of them will ever make it, let alone be remembered for what they did on the football field.

"As the weeks go by, you start to form friendships with the other guys trying to make the team. You see them, one by one, either leaving or getting cut. Then you look around in the meeting on Monday and go, 'Whoa, there are a lot fewer people in here today than there were last Monday.' And, if you're lucky—and strong—you might be able to say, 'I'm still here. I'm still here.'"

Head Down Doesn't Mean Eyes Shut

"When you're a rookie trying to make the team, the veterans don't warm up to you. No one—not even you—knows how long you'll be around," says Drew Pearson. "It's bad luck to attach yourself to a guy and then wake up one morning to discover he's gone. Who wants to make new friends, only to watch them disappear?

"So out of self-preservation, the veterans were more than a little standoffish. We wouldn't socialize with the rookies. We were coming off a Super Bowl win and were one of the favorites going into the 1978 season. The Cowboys roster was one of the most difficult in the league to crack.

"We had drafted Tony Hill in 1977, and he became a starter the following year. And Golden Richards was on the team then. Turns out that Robert moved into that spot when he made the roster.

"We all learned a lesson from Robert, who just kept his head down and kept plugging away. Even if you're a rookie at the bottom of the list, don't make the mistake of thinking you haven't got a chance. It doesn't matter where you rank, or whether you're first or last. What matters is that you're in the game, and you've got one chance to show the coaches—or your bosses, or your spouse, or your teachers, or your parents—what you've got.

"Do your best regardless of where you rank. If you're at the bottom of the list, keep in mind that you're not going to stay there forever. As others drop out for one reason or another, you'll find yourself moving up in rank, especially if you continue to give it your best shot. Pretty soon, you won't be in last place anymore. In time, you might surprise yourself and even reach that top spot. So always play as though you're already Number One.

"Don't let the veterans intimidate you. Learn from them without being distracted or afraid of their rank and status. You can learn a lot by watching the pros and imitating what they're doing right.

"Stand out by performing your job to the best of your ability. Put in the extra time. Go that extra mile. When you're doing your job—and you should expect that all eyes are on you all the time—stay focused on the task at hand. Don't get distracted. Keep doing your job as if everything depends on it—because it does!"

And never underestimate the value of common courtesy and a friendly gesture, like sharing your grandmother's pound cake!

7

Paying My Dues

Dan and Dana Reeves

One warm, sunny afternoon at camp, I was minding my own business, riding my bike across campus on the way to the players' dorm. When I reached the end of the pavement, I jumped off my bike—and ran right into square-jawed Coach Dan Reeves.

Originally from Americus, Georgia, just south of my hometown of Columbus, Reeves played quarterback at the University of South Carolina but began his NFL career as a free-agent running back for the Cowboys. Over eight seasons, he gained a reputation as a versatile team player, a hard-nosed runner who could also catch and pass the ball. (Reeves's claim to fame is a touchdown pass he threw to Lance Rentzel in the "Ice Bowl" game, immortalized in Jerry Kramer's memoir *Instant Replay*, against Green Bay in the 1967 NFL Championship game.)

The Cowboys did that a lot—first find a player with some skill and the desire to win, and then find a position for that player to play. Today it's commonplace—draft experts call it

BAA (choosing the "best athlete available")—but more than forty years ago, the Cowboys were on the cutting edge when it came to filling out rosters. That was certainly encouraging to me, to see how players made their way in the league under similar circumstances to what I was going through.

Coach Reeves never said much to me during camp, so I was surprised when he wanted to talk to me.

"I'm sick and tired of hearing your name," he said sternly, standing in front of me with his arms crossed. Although I was three or four inches taller than he was, he cut an intimidating figure. At the time, he would only have been in his mid-thirties and a handful of years from his playing days. Plus, he was one of the coaches who would decide when it came time whether or not I made the team.

"Excuse me?" I tried a nonchalant laugh that sounded more like a cat being strangled and thought, just for an instant, that my professional football career—the one that hadn't even started yet—might be coming to an abrupt close.

"I said, 'I'm sick and tired of hearing your name.'" No change in expression.

"Coach, I don't know what you're talking about. What have I done?"

"Every night when I call home to speak to my wife, Pam, she puts my twelve-year-old daughter, Dana, on the phone. I want to ask my daughter about what she's doing this summer—going to camp, hanging out with her friends—and all she wants to know is whether or not Robert Steele is still on the team. She doesn't even want to talk to her daddy. And I'm sick and tired of it."

For the first time in our conversation, I caught a hint of a smile in his voice. He was giving me a hard time, but at least he wasn't there to do the Turk's job.

"Coach, I don't know your daughter, but I think she's a brilliant young lady." Now that I knew he was messing with me,

I laughed. I was flattered that Reeves would take the time to approach me. "You know, children are the best judges of character. You should listen to Dana."

"Yeah, we'll see about that!" He laughed—a good, honest laugh—and shooed me away with a wave of his hand.

I was comforted to know that my first fan, the coach's daughter, kept an admiring eye on my progress.

Football gets in a person's blood, and I heard later that Dana eventually married a coach. Years later, I met Dana's husband, the special teams coach for the Atlanta Falcons, where Dan Reeves was the head coach. I told him the story of twelve-year-old Dana and her precocious football wisdom.

"Sounds a lot like Dana," Joe said, shaking his head. "She always did know more about football than anybody I've ever met. What's not to love!"

"I knew when Dan pulled me aside and told me that story," I said, "that she must have been one smart cookie. Be sure to tell Dana, from the bottom of my heart, that I really appreciated her support."

North Dallas Forty

One Sunday afternoon halfway through camp, we were given a night off. Big news, since we had been working our butts off without a break and, to a man, the team was exhausted. The only stipulation was that we spend our time off with the same guys that we saw on the field every day.

Not ideal, but fair enough.

We boarded buses and headed into the movie theater in Camarillo, California, to watch *North Dallas Forty*, a film starring Nick Nolte, Mac Davis, and Charles Durning. Since its wide release in 1979, it's become a cult classic with sports fans.

The movie presented an image of a Dallas team from an

earlier time, leading the viewer to believe that this was what life in pro football really was like. I never saw or lived *that* picture.

Yes, there were drugs around.

Yes, the influences and temptations of the day ruined many players.

The best thing director Pete Gent did in portraying the Dallas Cowboys in *North Dallas Forty*, though, was to show that America's Team was made up of real people, people with the same problems the rest of society faced every day when they rolled out of bed. In the case of the players, football was their job, and they did their jobs with passion and gusto.

Overall, the movie had many true-to-life parts—as well as a few "Hollywood" effects—and it was a great experience, watching a movie loosely based *on* the Dallas Cowboys *with* the Dallas Cowboys. In the theater, I sat directly behind Roger Staubach, who was portrayed by Mac Davis in the film as a straight arrow.

Roger's character was pretty much spot-on. Who else would tell Chevrolet he wanted a station wagon instead of the flashy 'Vette when he won Most Valuable Player in the Super Bowl?

But Roger knew who he was and what he wanted out of life, and he didn't let Hollywood—or anybody, for that matter— change who he was. I hadn't spent much time with Roger except on the practice field, but I could see his devotion to everything he did. As I got to know him more later on, I came to realize that he was one of the most consistent individuals I'd ever met, strong in his core beliefs and comfortable enough with himself to always make decisions that he could live with.

We should all be as secure in our identity as Roger Staubach.

On the ride back to campus, the team gave Roger plenty of grief for being Mr. Goody Two-Shoes. Despite the kidding, every player admired Roger and what he stood for. He was the one sports figure that America could look up to—the All-American boy playing for America's Team.

Clothing Optional

It's no revelation that part of the rite of initiation for a rookie in camp is to be hassled by the veterans (see above: *North Dallas Forty*). One Sunday afternoon late in training camp, Randy White and Randy Hughes invited me to go to for a ride up along the coast in their rented car. Sounded harmless enough.

"Sure," was all I could muster, my voice cracking. I was so intimidated by the veterans that if they told me to jump off a building, I would have said, "Just tell me where to land."

Hughes and White waited for me in the parking lot. Randy White, affectionately known as the Manster—half man, half monster—was one of the few people in the world I truly feared. He always looked as if he wanted to take off your head. In fact, when I got in the backseat of the car that day, he jumped into the front seat, turned around to face me, and snarled.

I just sat there, never said two words, and listened in awe to these seasoned veterans talk about football. I should have known I was in trouble when they stopped the car on the side of a road facing a long slope down to the ocean and got out. I didn't join them right away, just sat there some more and weighed my few options. We were miles from the nearest town or a pay phone—who was I going to call anyway?—so I slid out of the car.

White motioned me over to the ledge. He was standing beside a weather-beaten wooden sign at the entrance to a narrow dirt path that ran down to the ocean. I took a closer look as the two stifled laughs behind their hands.

N de Bea h This W y ➜

"Come on, rookie," White said, grabbing me by the shirt.

"A nude beach?" I stood there and laughed, kind of an aw-shucks thing that came out of nowhere. I really had no idea of how I was going to get out of this.

"Sure. Come on, Rook."

"They have nude beaches here? I thought that was only in Europe."

Despite my protest, White and Hughes picked their way down the slope. I could see people in the distance, batting a volleyball around and splashing at the water's edge. As we got closer, I could see—a little too clearly, for a raw kid out of Columbus, Georgia—that no one had on a stitch of clothing. We walked around a big dune protecting the beach and saw five hundred naked bodies—none of them what I imagined when I thought of Southern California beaches—taking advantage of sun.

"Take your shorts off," Hughes said. It was more of a command than an invitation, and I realized that we had finally gotten to the hazing ritual.

"No way," I shot back. "I don't care if you guys do, but I'm not doing it."

White and Hughes looked at each other and shrugged their shoulders, not in the mood to take the joke any further than they already had. We stood there glancing at the naked bodies (well, I was probably staring at some point on the horizon; believe me, it wasn't a pretty sight) and chatted about the absurdity of the whole idea of naked sunbathing. There was one bright spot to the day. There was this Bo Derek–looking young woman frolicking in the water and seemed to be enjoying every minute being "free as a bird." Hughes spent the better part of our time watching her, and I could tell White didn't really care either way.

They were testing me. When we left a few minutes later, I listened intently to their conversation. They felt like they had "made a man out of me" by taking me to the nude beach.

It took me a few days to get over seeing so many naked, ugly bodies on that beach. *Never want to do that again*, I thought as we drove back to the to the Cal Lutheran campus. *All I want to do is focus on making the team. All other distractions are just that, distractions.*

Why did they invite me to go?

These were two defensive, not offensive, players. One was a defensive lineman and one a defensive back, so I wasn't a threat to them or their jobs.

Why did I go with them, even though I suspected something was up?

Since I got along with almost every player, this was one more opportunity to blend. The better we knew each other, the more accepting they became of my efforts.

After four weeks at camp, guys started to reach out to one another. We had come so far together and were so close to making the team that we had closed ranks. All the draftees and free agents had survived many cuts, and the coaches judged our performances harshly all day, every day. Those rookies like me still in camp had come a long way from where we first started.

By inviting me to join them on the nude beach, White and Hughes—two of the most respected players on the team— showed that they cared enough to give me a hard time. In hindsight, I understand that the only thing worse than having to join them on the beach was not being invited at all, which probably would have meant that I was on the next plane out of LAX, winging my way back to Atlanta and the life of a recent college graduate.

The invitation was their way of saying, *We respect how far you've come, how quickly you've made progress.*

Or maybe they were really saying, *There might be a chance for your skinny butt yet, Steele.*

Giving Back—and Getting Back

Because Cal Lutheran College allowed the Cowboys to rent their facilities for a few weeks every summer, the Cowboys hosted several social events throughout the season to show their

The phrase instantly became my newfound trademark and continues to be: "*Steele: Here?* Why are you *Steele here?*"

About seven years ago while I was in a board meeting, my executive assistant interrupted to inform me that Bob Walters, the CFO for one of my investors, was on the phone. Bob normally didn't interrupt a meeting unless it was urgent, so I told my assistant I would call him back as soon as we could take a break.

Seconds later, in a room full of executives, she interrupted the meeting again and said, "This is important. Bob wants to be put on speaker phone."

I didn't know what to expect.

"Robert, sorry to interrupt. Got a minute?" His tone of voice told me it wasn't an emergency, and I wondered why he would interrupt me. "I'm on an airplane and have someone here who really wants to say hello."

A split-second later, I was taken back to August 1978.

"*Steele here?* Why are you *Steele here?*" That was all I needed to hear. I recognized the voice immediately. Drew always had a voice that was unique. When he spoke, I always tried to catch every word. Drew was so secure within himself that he took time to teach us rookies even when he was tired from practicing as well. So, when I heard the voice, I knew who it was. With a deep laugh, Drew Pearson, who was sitting next to Bob in first class on a plane back to Dallas, took me back twenty-five years to that great moment.

I never forgot "Steele here." And Drew hadn't either.

Many friends of mine in the business community have hired Drew to speak to their group. Drew is an accomplished speaker and can move a crowd with his stories of the Cowboys. Jon McBride, the CTO from Availity, hired Drew as well not long ago to speak to their company. After the speech, Jon asked Drew if he remembered Robert Steele. Drew continues to say, "Don't remember Robert Steele, but I remember Steele Here."

Red Zone Rules

Under Pressure

"Football is a deceptively complex game because you have so many things you're up against. Sure, the physical aspects, but also the mental game, like always getting into position, knowing your role on the field, and working to make it through training camp, which is always more mental than physical. Peer pressure is also a big part of the game, but not many people ever talk about it," says Bruce Huther.

"The other players at your position don't want you to make the team, they want to hold on to their jobs. Many, many players vie for every open roster spot, and peer pressure—or the ability to understand peer pressure and manage it—often separates the nows from the has-beens."

The Best Medicine

Thank your supporters, whoever they may be. Let them know how much you appreciate them. You may not be able to repay them, but you can always "pay it forward."

How?

- Give back to your community.

- Extend a helping hand to others.

- Maintain your discipline. Distractions and temptations will pop up, but you've got to hold on to your values.

- Stay on the straight and narrow. Be aware of your surroundings, but never lose that tunnel vision that will help you to reach your ultimate goal.

- Work hard, but don't take yourself too seriously. Let some humor into your life. It's OK to laugh with a coach, your peers, your competitors, your bosses, and your colleagues now and then.

- Make the most of those light moments—they relieve tension and unite everyone in a common goal. "We had fun, even in practice," recalls Bruce Huther. "We would laugh, kid around. You don't picture that in the Landry system. But it's a necessary part of winning, that ability to keep things in perspective."

8

Long Odds

"A million to one. . . ."

By the third week in August, the Thousand Oaks training camp was about to break. Final cuts were coming. I had managed to survive "the Turk" every time, but I knew my chances of making the final cut still weren't good.

A free agent making the World Champion Cowboys? Give me a break.

It was a rare moment when I allowed such a question or doubt to creep into my thoughts, but the reality was that so few players made the roster as free agents that I would've been better off driving to Las Vegas and betting my future on a spin of the roulette wheel or a toss of the dice.

"Will the team keep five receivers?" I asked Mike Ditka before practice one afternoon.

Ditka—like Tony Dorsett, a Pittsburgh guy—was a Hall of Fame tight end for the Chicago Bears (he finished his career with the Philadelphia Eagles and Dallas, where he was on the winning side in Super Bowl VI). Later, of course, he would become legendary as the coach of "Da Bears" and the idol of a pack of rabid, beer-swilling fans on *Saturday Night Live*. A fearsome presence even during his college career at the University of Pittsburgh, Ditka was hired as an assistant by Coach Landry after retiring in 1972.

To say that his reputation preceded him would be to diminish the effect he had on players, especially ones who hadn't made the team yet.

"Never have before, but there's always a first time," he said, in a voice so gruff it made my throat hurt. Ditka was always a direct guy, and I wouldn't have expected him to blow happy smoke at me about my chances of making the team, but his response didn't make me feel any better. It did mean, though, that the team might be thinking about keeping five wide receivers for the first time.

Possibly.

Maybe.

The magnitude of what I was up against really hit home in one of those rare quiet moments in the locker room. I was sitting on the bench by myself trying to gather my thoughts before practice when one of my teammates threw a newspaper in my face.

"What do you think about this?" he said with a smirk.

I let the paper drop to the locker room floor. "What do I think about what?"

"Have you read today's newspaper?"

"I haven't read a newspaper since I got to Dallas in the spring. Who the hell has time? My name isn't in there anyway. . . ."

"You're wrong. Here." He picked the paper up off the floor and neatly folded it back to the sports section. He pointed about halfway down the page, and I caught a glimpse of my name.

"They're saying you've got a million to one shot of making the team. I didn't say you'd *like* what they had to say. I just said your name was in the paper."

"Well, that's good news." I felt like the guy who had brought me the paper was having a laugh at my expense. The handful of guys who had come around to see what the commotion was about just rolled their eyes at our exchange.

"Good news?"

"Yeah. At least that means I got one shot. I'm OK with that."

Would I take those odds?

You bet!

As long as I had a uniform—even a rookie's—I knew I had a shot.

That's the name of the game. And I'm going to go out there and just do my job.

Steele here!

Because of that newspaper clipping—or maybe in spite of it—I was inspired to rise to the next level of effort for the next couple of weeks, which is exactly what I needed to do.

We flew into Dallas for the final preseason game against Houston on a Saturday night in Texas Stadium. What a fun way for me to go out, if this was going to be my swan song. I could envision making a catch in Texas Stadium, the highlight of the evening—hell, the highlight of my career.

Yes, indeed. Steele here!

I knew Sunday would be a long, hard day because it was either my last as a Cowboy or my last as a free agent. I had done everything I could do. Moving up the depth chart, catching almost every pass, playing special teams, running extra pass routes for any quarterback who needed the extra work—all my way of proving that I belonged in the NFL.

I did everything I could—and I was confident that I had given my best effort over the previous two months—but million-to-one odds meant only one thing: I had a chance, and that was all.

Special Teams Practice

Having played wide receiver in college and being a starter for my last two seasons meant I didn't have to play on special teams. Special teams—kickoffs, punts, extra point and field goal attempts—are an important part of football. Statistically, almost a third of the plays in a game are on special teams. Watch a slate of NFL matchups on any given Sunday and you realize that one play—a bad snap, a missed block, a muffed punt, a ball that rolls dead on the two-yard-line or bounces into the end zone for a touchback—can change not only a single game, but a team's season.

My only experience with special teams was holding for extra points and field goals in college and kicking them in high school. Being on the "suicide squad," as some people labeled special teams—for the reckless abandon with which blockers and tacklers ran full-force into one another in the game's most chaotic and violent collisions—never appealed to me. But when I asked about what I could do to increase my chances of making the team, a coach told me that one proven method was to play special teams.

Would I sacrifice my body on the kickoff, punt coverage, and kick return teams?

Stupid question! Hadn't I told a doctor earlier in the summer that I would jump out of a skyscraper window to make the team?

I didn't hesitate to join the special teams when I was told that might give me an edge.

The one thing going for me was that Coach Ditka was also the special teams coach. He may have been mean as a snake and only liked "killers" on his coverage teams, but he was also the one who told me that to have a realistic chance of making the team, I needed to make myself indispensible—and I could do that by playing special teams.

I asked Ditka if I could join him.

"You're on the dummy squad, Steele," Ditka rasped, with the emphasis on *dummy*. "Not special teams. You've got to earn that."

Ditka's words stung me. For the first time, I felt my chances dwindle.

While we prepared for our first game in Texas Stadium, just a few weeks before, against the San Francisco 49ers, a team starring an aging O. J. Simpson in his last NFL season, Ditka set up blocking schemes for the punt-protection team. He called the dummy squad out to rush the punter, backup quarterback Danny White. The purpose of the drill was to make sure that White could regularly get the ball away in less than 2.2 seconds. Punt blocking is an important skill, and Ditka knew getting the release time down was crucial. Anything much over two seconds, and the punt would be blocked—a serious mistake that could lead to a shift in the game's momentum.

On the first snap, I charged from the right end. Within a split-second, I was on top of White, ready to block the kick. Ditka got red in the face, hollered a few unmentionable phrases, and shouted, with barely controlled rage, "Let's do it again."

The next time, I went to the left side and waited for the snap. Untouched, I flew around the left end and rushed White, getting to the ball almost before he could snatch it out of the air.

Ditka lost his mind.

"Steele beat you again? You stupid bastards are going to keep doing this until you drop. We've got San Francisco coming up, and you can't block a guy on the dummy squad. What the hell are you going to do against real NFL players?"

I must have had a smile on my face, because when Ditka turned toward me in the middle of his outburst, looking at me seemed to make him even angrier.

All the commotion got Coach Landry's attention. He motioned Ditka and Reeves over, and the three talked for a minute, Ditka gesturing and pointing my direction in a spittle-flecked tirade.

When the meeting broke up, the defensive coaches got involved.

"Steele, go up the middle. Block it this time, and Ditka will be *furious*." I lined up over center and waited for the snap. I got a real kick out of the glee the defensive coaches displayed when they imagined just how upset Ditka would be.

I got a good jump on the snap and brushed the center out of the way, going untouched again to White. On my way past the punter—the third time in three tries—I stole a glance at Ditka, who threw his clipboard to the ground, swore under his breath, and stalked over to the group of guys watching the play.

The next time, he lined five blockers up against me. It was the only time I didn't get to the punter.

The coaches had noticed me. On Saturday, I was on the punt-block team in Texas Stadium in front of sixty thousand fans for my first preseason game. I had gone from scout team to special teams in two-and-a-half days. If I could do that, I decided, then the coaches must want me on the field. I wondered what the odds were at that point. Certainly better than a million-to-one.

I had an extra adrenaline boost when, right before kickoff, Charlie Waters came up to me and said, "Coach Landry wants you to hold for extra points now."

"Doesn't Coach Landry need to come and tell me that?" I asked, excited but guarded. Rumors tended to run rampant in training camp, and I didn't want to have my hopes dashed.

"No, Robert, I've already talked to him. You're going to hold for extra points."

And in that moment, I also became the holder.

In our last four days in Thousand Oaks and our last week in Dallas, we were down to sixty players—fifteen over the opening-day roster. The rookie locker room was deathly quiet and, frankly, not much fun. Any banter we had shared earlier in camp, any camaraderie we had begun to feel for guys who shared a common goal—that was gone and replaced by guys who just sat around waiting for the other shoe to drop.

A couple of particularly superstitious players stopped taking phone calls, even from family members who had been tracking their progress throughout camp, because they were convinced that the Turk might try to call them rather than tapping them on the foot in the morning and delivering those dreaded words: "Coach Landry wants to see you. Bring your playbook."

Everybody still in camp looked at himself in the mirror and thought—or at least hoped against hope—that he was *the one,* the free agent who would make it to Opening Day.

A week after a teammate had thrown a newspaper in my face, he was sent packing.

I was Steele here.

And the odds were a million to one.

"The Catch"

Having made an impression with my ability to catch a football, I was pleased to be alternating with Drew Pearson, the team's star receiver, just weeks after having been last on the rookie depth chart. We were headed back to Texas Stadium to play the Houston Oilers for our final preseason game. It was my last shot to shine.

Final cuts were coming Monday, the day after the game. On Wednesday afternoon, prior to breaking camp in Thousand Oaks and heading home to Dallas, we ran a relatively informal practice, working on plays for the game that weekend. Our best plays were the "three-route," a four-step-and-out route, our bread-and-butter calls whenever we needed a first down.

By the end of the day, we had run just about every play in the book. I knew we were getting close to the day's end, because the scouts moved toward the other end of the field, where we gathered to run wind sprints. I watched as Tony Dorsett scampered around the right side for a big gain, making it look effortless as usual.

The next play was a pass to me, a three-route. I knew what to do—what I had practiced all summer and could duplicate in my sleep (in fact I had, on many occasions, gotten awake with my legs pumping under the sheets and sweat on my brow as if I had really been running the pass plays that I dreamed about). If Roger Staubach threw the ball my way, I knew I would catch it.

When he let rip, the ball was high and wide. I stretched out and, without thinking, made a one-handed catch—right in front of Coach Landry's face—and tiptoed out of bounds. I nonchalantly trotted back to the huddle and got ready for the next play.

Before I knew it, Coach Landry blew the final whistle and called the team together to run wind sprints—ten 110-yard sprints that seemed to take forever at the end of a long day of practice. Although my lungs burned like fire at the end of the drill, I enjoyed feeling the strength in my legs, the endorphins rushing to my brain. I was especially inspired on this last day of training camp, though, because Coach Landry said a few words to the team and then, looking right at me, said, "Good practice and great catch, Steele. See you at dinner."

A stunned team looked around, and a smile graced every player's face as many of them ran to the locker room to shower and prepare for dinner.

At the end of camp, only five rookies made the team: Alois Blackwell, Dennis Thurman, Larry Bethea, Tom Randall, and me, the only free agent out of the eighty who started camp—and a man who had the indescribable pleasure of realizing a dream.

Pass–Catch Ratio

During training camp, the Cowboys kept statistics on everything. Players joked that they kept stats on how many times a day we tied our shoes or how many trips we made to the buffet during lunch.

They also paid close attention to who was ten or fifteen minutes early to practice. Of course, no one was ever late.

The scouts were hard to miss, walking officiously from group to group and recording their observations on their omnipresent clipboards like managers at a car-parts factory. I was surprised when I got wind at the end of training camp that I had the best "pass–catch" ratio in camp (and, I heard later, maybe of all time). Every time a quarterback threw me a pass in drills, passing sessions, or scrimmages, a scout recorded who threw the ball, whether the ball was caught, and by whom.

When it came time to grade players for the cuts, the scouts—and the coaches, of course, once the information was digested and presented to them—knew the stats on everybody wearing a uniform. My pass–catch ratio earned me the nickname "Flypaper" from Bruce Huther, a linebacker who had made the team a year earlier as a free agent. Bruce's line was, "If it comes near him, the ball seems to stick to him." I felt great because my peers had noticed.

And I knew that a good reputation, especially one given me by a defensive player, didn't hurt my chances of grabbing the coaches' attention.

Red Zone Rules

No "I" in T-E-A-M

"There was a really nice article a while back in *Fortune* magazine about how hard work is the surest path to success. That's true, of course, but you've got to work smart, too, put time and effort into anything you do," says Roger Staubach.

"A lot of that time and effort and hard work can overcome just about any shortcomings. Or if you're an athlete, you can perform and accomplish more than players who might even have more talent than you, because you're giving it that total effort.

"You've got to have the basics, and Robert certainly had that aspect of the game down cold. He caught the ball very well. Physically, he was a big guy, a rangy guy—never a bad trait from a quarterback's perspective, because he could go up and get the ball from smaller defensive backs—and he had a tremendous work ethic. We were probably as good as any football team in the league at that time. We also had a real teamwork mentality. I think that's an important characteristic, to make sure you put the overall success of your team ahead of your own personal goals.

"Robert definitely was a team player."

High-Attitude Flying

To achieve your dream, you have to go full speed every day. I'm not talking about burning yourself out (see above and Roger Staubach's admonition to work hard *and* smart), but you've got to focus on the task at hand and make the most of every moment.

Never dawdle or waste time.

Learn.

Stay involved.

You've got to give 100 percent effort—every single time on the field—and you need to do it with a positive attitude.

Nobody likes a complainer. Maintain an upbeat disposition, for those around you—and for yourself. You can achieve much more with a positive attitude than with a negative outlook.

Timing is everything.

Until the time is right and it's your turn to shine—practice, practice, practice! That way, you'll be ready when your moment finally arrives.

You make friends by being friendly. A friendly disposition wins people to your side every time. I found this to be true in the Cowboys' cutthroat world, where we walked the razor's edge each day—and you'll find it's just as true in whatever you do.

Man on a Mission

"Robert didn't mind getting his hands dirty. He would do the little things, the nasty things, the things that took lots of work and sweat. He was tough, tenacious, resilient. He ran his routes with the attention to detail of a watchmaker," recalls Charlie Waters.

"As a matter of fact, he endeared himself with me because I used to run the defense. When Robert's practice squad would run the other team's offense for us, Robert would always come to me and ask me if he was doing the right things.

Is this the way they do it?

Maybe you can tell me how I can give my practice-squad guys a better picture of what they run.

"Now that's a guy who thinks like a coach, a CEO, a big-picture player who understands the concept of team and how to win games. I held him in high regard because of that.

"I knew it was a long shot for him to make it in the NFL. There are great stories like that. Everybody who's made it—*everybody*—has overcome some serious hurdles.

"From the first day, you could tell those sorts of issues weren't going to derail Robert, that he was a man on a mission and wouldn't be denied."

9

The Crucible

Battle for the Great State of Texas

By late August, the Cowboys had played three of their four pre-season games, and the rosters were all but set for the 1978 season. What seemed like a cast of thousands at the outset of camp eight weeks before had been trimmed to fifty—five short of the forty-five-man Opening Day roster. The final preseason game against the Houston Oilers was an intrastate rivalry played for the Governor's Cup, the championship of Texas.

The two teams had played many preseason games, but the 1978 season was special. For one thing, it was the rookie season for one of the most anticipated debuts in NFL memory, the arrival of running back Earl Campbell. Campbell, a University of Texas superstar who had won the Heisman trophy at the end of the previous winter's college football season, was big, he was fast, and he ran around and over players with a glee—and an apparent ease—that hadn't been seen before in the NFL. In his senior season at Texas, Campbell had amassed 1,700 yards rushing. More than 800 of those yards were YAC, or "yards after contact."

In other words, Earl was a bruiser who made the defense pay every time he touched the ball. Cliff Harris had a classic quote in the *Dallas Morning News* as we prepared to take on Campbell and the Oilers, who had been challenging the Pittsburgh Steelers for supremacy in the AFC: "Every time you tackle Earl Campbell, your IQ goes down ten points."

In addition to Campbell's introduction to Dallas, the coaches prepared to make final cuts, which would be announced on the Monday after the Houston game. The coaches and scouts would spend the entire day on Sunday discussing five or six players and who would stay and who would go.

My Sunday was spent nursing wounds from the night before. Actually, I was in pretty good shape from the game, though I spent much of the afternoon worrying about what was going to happen.

Would today be the day I met the Turk?

The Cowboys would open their season the following week against the Baltimore Colts, and my future hung in the balance—I would either be a professional football player gearing up for the season of my life, or another has-been sent home to watch the NFL on television.

When I didn't get a call on Sunday, I knew Monday would be the day.

Monday morning passed. No phone call.

Had I made it? No news is good news, right?

I didn't have to wait much longer to find out. Around noon on Monday, the phone in my hotel room rang. Gil Brandt was on the line.

"Robert, are you available to come next door?"

The Cowboys headquarters was located on Central Expressway, next door to the Ramada Inn, where players lodged during the preseason. Walking next door meant crossing the parking lot, and even though I would be in Gil's office in less than five minutes, I had way too much time to think about what would happen when I got there.

Gil hadn't ask for my playbook, so maybe they weren't cutting me, nor had he said anything about meeting with Coach Landry.

Am I on the team or about to be sent home? If the Cowboys cut me, will another team really want me, like Cornell told me that first night in Florence at Dale's Restaurant?

I was the fifth wide receiver for the last preseason game. Of course, that's when I remembered my conversation with Ditka about my chances. His hemming and hawing hadn't really inspired confidence. Although it had never happened, there could always be a first time. NFL roster spots are so precious, though, that there has to be a compelling reason why the team might carry an extra player at a position.

I found out that Dave Kraayeveld had been cut the day before and was already on a plane to Seattle. He had been picked up by the Seattle Seahawks, which reminded me of a conversation with Cornell on the night I signed my contract.

I saw how the roster was taking shape. Tony Hill was pressing Golden Richards for more playing time as the team geared up for opening day against Baltimore. I was confused. Gil's call didn't seem to be consistent with what I thought to be the process.

All this in the two minutes it took to walk across the parking lot. The unanswered questions ran through my mind, and I remember even ticking them off on my fingers as Gil's office got closer. My gut felt like someone was pulling a fishing hook through my intestines.

Gil waved me in.

"Mr. Brandt, I'm not sure of the process, but I think I know why I'm here." I stuffed my hands in my pockets to keep them from shaking. Gil gave me a consoling look that suggested he had been through this before—probably many times.

"Robert! Thanks for coming over. First of all, I want to congratulate you on an outstanding training camp and for making it this far. You've worked your ass off, and everybody in the organization appreciates the effort and the dedication you've brought to the Cowboys. We're a better team for your having been here these past eight weeks."

I didn't know exactly how he was going to let me down, but I could see disappointment coming down the expressway with its doors open. His next words hit me like a ton of bricks.

"Robert, we're placing you on waivers. I'm not at liberty to tell you everything going on behind the scenes, but let me give you at least a glimmer of hope. We're trying to work something out. We'd like for you to go home, see your family. Let's wait and see if something works out." He reached out and shook my hand. I wasn't even shaking anymore, just mentally wrung out from the anticipation of the meeting, and I grabbed his hand and thanked him for his and the team's time.

Go home? See what works out? What does that mean? How long am I waiting?

More questions with no answers.

Gil did ask me to go and retrieve my playbook. I would be whisked off to the airport to catch a flight back to Atlanta and make the ride down to Columbus. Gil's only order was simple. He told me to stay near the house.

Was that the request that passed for hopeful, to stay close to a phone?

His final words landed with a hollow thud: "We'll be in touch."

It was the third time this summer I had heard that phrase—the worst kind of brush-off—and I remember thinking on the way back to the hotel that even to discover that I hadn't made the team might have been more comforting, in a weird way, than waiting for the Cowboys to "be in touch"—again. I called my parents and told them the news as I got my playbook together for the last walk over.

The Waiting Game

My parents picked me up at the airport. Going back home and staying with my parents was both a blessing and a curse. I had failed. My million-to-one shot had turned out to be a blank, a dud. I had missed my target.

But I had come close. Damn close.

I sat on my hands in Columbus for the next seven days to keep from toying with the phone. Mentally, the week was the most difficult of my life.

Are you going to call today, or am I done forever?

I had way too much time on my hands, and a million thoughts—most of them bad—ran through my mind:

What did "We'll be in touch" mean? Was that a kind way of letting me down?

Gil hinted that something might happen. Nothing was going to happen. None of the receivers were going to get hurt.

I'm a mental mess. I did everything I knew how to do to put myself in position to succeed, and this is what I get for my effort.

I know I belong. Playing for the Cowboys is my destiny.

It's a good thing I have my college degree.

I should be practicing with the team. I deserve it.

What do you mean, "Sit back and wait and see what might happen"?

Obviously, waiting wasn't my strong suit.

Tuesday, Wednesday, Thursday, passed without a peep.

Friday came and went.

Saturday and Sunday felt like years crawling by—and I was beginning to get on my parents' nerves. Trying to watch the pro games on Sunday waiting for Monday to come seemed like a fog I was in without knowing if the fog would ever lift.

Monday wasn't much better.

I was losing hope. I knew that I had to change my negative thinking fast before I sank into depression.

Instead of continuing to worry, I started asking myself positive questions.

Why are the Cowboys keeping my name?

If Kraayeveld got picked up by Seattle, then will I? What could possibly "work out"?

Am I available if another team member is hurt?

Game night arrived. Monday Night Football featured the Dallas Cowboys and the Baltimore Colts on national television, Howard Cosell and Dandy Don Meredith in the booth. As much as I felt I deserved to be on that field, I was still in Columbus watching the game with my parents in their den. Not what I had expected or even hoped for. I had come a long way, but then the irony of my situation was that I hadn't moved an inch since graduating from North Alabama in May.

I had begun my journey in Columbus, Georgia, and I seemed destined to end it there.

Game time was 9:00 p.m., and the announcers ran through the starting line-ups, noting how the new season brought a few minor changes. Golden Richards wouldn't be starting— Tony Hill, the outstanding prospect from Stanford, would take his place—but other than that, business as usual for America's Team. The television cameras panned the Cowboys sideline throughout the game. Coach Landry, in his trademark fedora and the disposition of a man in control of every aspect of the game, got plenty of television time.

The game was progressing as usual: the Cowboys were winning and my "teammates" were playing very well. Oddly, though, no Golden on the field. The camera caught him on the sidelines sitting on his helmet. Golden had started Super Bowl XII eight months before, and he was contracted to make

$100,000 for the 1978 season. Apparently much of that salary would be drawn for sitting on his helmet.

Why not me?

I looked at Mom next to me on the couch.

"That means something," I told her, with as much hope in my voice as I could muster.

"Maybe they're going to make a trade," Dad chimed in. "Or cut him." I knew Dad may have been right, since the coaches and the front office wouldn't leave Golden sitting on his helmet all season.

Just then, my thoughts returned to the positive. I could almost hear Gil's voice.

Let's wait and see if something works out.

Maybe my dad was right? Would the Cowboys trade the fan favorite, the golden boy?

Something was about to pop. I could feel it. I had a hard time sleeping that night as the possibilities raced through my mind.

Brandt "Works Something Out"

At ten o'clock the next morning, Gil Brandt finally called.

"Robert, how are you?" I knew Gil was the best in the business at what he did—evaluate and manage talent—but I wished I could have read his voice a little better. He was a master at never giving anything away, either in person or on the phone.

"I'm fine, Mr. Brandt. I was hoping I'd hear from you some-time . . . soon."

"Did you watch the game last night?"

"Of course! Wish I could've been there." As excited as I was to hear from him, I tried to keep the disappointment out of my voice over having to watch my team on television rather than being in the trenches.

Gil picked up on my tone and cut the small talk.

"Listen, let me get to the point. Are you available to come to Dallas today?"

After everything I had been through, the best I could muster, was, "Ah, yeah. Dallas? Today?"

"Good news. We've traded Golden Richards to the Bears to make a roster spot for you."

I stood there in my parents' living room just holding the phone like an idiot. Gil filled the silence.

"We need you on the practice field—now, today. We play the New York Giants this coming Sunday. I've already checked the airlines. There's a flight leaving Atlanta at two o'clock. You'll get here by three Central. That'll give you just enough time to make the four o'clock practice."

"Fantastic! I'm there. If I have to run all the way, I'm there."

"Are you sure you don't need some time to pack?" He laughed with me, and I was laughing at myself, acting like a kid who had just found a new bike under the Christmas tree.

"I haven't unpacked my bags, Mr. Brandt. You told me to be ready. I'm ready."

I practically hung up the phone on him so I could go grab my bag—it was in exactly the same place I had dropped seven days before—and head to the airport, about an hour and a half northeast of Columbus.

I didn't even have time to celebrate with my family. I figured if I needed anything else, I'd just buy it later. I was about to receive my five grand "making the team" bonus—modest as it was—that the Cowboys had never anticipated paying out.

I was flying so high, I didn't need Delta to get me to Dallas. Gil had sent a driver who waited for me at the Dallas–Fort Worth airport, and next thing I knew, I was in a limo cruising to the Cowboys practice facility—my first time there as a member of the Dallas Cowboys.

Red Zone Rules

Cleaning House

"When Tony Hill came in and took Golden's job, Coach Landry's philosophy was that when a starter loses his job to a backup, he doesn't keep the former starter around. That player becomes a detriment to the team," says Drew Pearson. "He becomes a negative, not a positive. So Golden, despite having started in the Super Bowl the year before, was traded to the Chicago Bears, and Tony was moved to the starting spot. The receivers were Tony Hill, Butch Johnson, and I—and 'Steele Here.'

"Who is that guy? He's Steele here."

Value Values

"Players will come in and give you everything they've got and still not make it. Maybe you have depth at that position, maybe the starter was just that little bit better. And in the end, you have to let that guy go. That's just the unfortunate reality of professional football," says Dan Reeves.

"When I talked to players we had to cut, I always told them, 'If you keep the same attitude you've got right now, you're going to be successful in life. That's what it's going to take, perseverance. You've got to keep working hard. If this is a dream, you'll get your chance.'

"Because we make the choices, that certainly doesn't mean we're always right. If we're releasing a player, somebody else who needs a strong guy at that position can get some real value from players who have been cut. We released Brian Billick earlier that year in camp and he went on to become the head coach of the Baltimore Ravens.

"The main thing is, regardless of the outcome, if a player gives full effort at football, he's going to be successful in life, in whatever he does. Robert is a great example of that. He's been successful in life because of the values he learned through football—in high school, college, and his time in the pros."

The Edge

Never lose hope. Even when you're at your lowest point and things are looking bleak, you have the power to replace those negative thoughts with positive ones. Hold on to that ability to think positively under all circumstances.

When the situation is uncertain, it's important that you stay flexible. You never know when you're going to get that call saying, "Come on over!" And if you're flexible enough to be ready when an opportunity presents itself, you've given yourself the edge.

10

#81

#81 On Your Program (#1 in Your Heart)

I had finally arrived. My name was printed on a placard on top of my locker with everything I would need to make it through the season. Beside my name was the number 81. I looked in my locker, and my name and number were already sewn onto the back of my jersey.

I was officially a member of the Dallas Cowboys—a rookie, sure, but a player nonetheless. Number 81 seemed like a good number. For some reason, I've always liked odd numbers. I wore 83 in high school, 87 and 89 in college, and 5 in baseball.

But who cares? I have a number!

An honest-to-God Dallas Cowboys jersey with my name on the back was all the physical proof I needed that I wasn't dreaming. No more rookie pants. I was still a rookie but a member of the team. My twenty-year-old rookie pants from training camp were not in my locker. We were all one team now, no more separation.

Teammates greeted me like it was old home week, and the place echoed with a dozen voices: "Steele's here. Steele's *still* here."

And then, from somewhere on the other side of the locker room after my first practice with the team: "Number 81 in your program, number 1 in your heart, Robert Steele." It was an old gag, but I embraced the sentiment. Every player there—even the guys who were a lot more talented than I was—had worked and sacrificed to make it, and I was overwhelmed to be a part of that group.

I was a rookie, no longer a free agent. I had made the team.

Coaches ran me in all the special teams' practices, and I was going to be on the punt return, kickoff coverage, and kickoff return teams.

After that first day of practice—real practice—I sat in front of my locker and allowed myself, just for an instant, to think about the journey I'd taken over the previous year.

A week ago, I was sitting with my parents in their den watching the Cowboys beat up on the Colts. This week, I'm preparing to play in the Meadowlands against the New York Giants, one of our most hated rivals.

Funny how things work sometimes.

Campisi's

Practice started at ten o'clock every morning. Gil Brandt asked me to come by his office prior to practice on Thursday. He handed me two names and phone numbers with the instructions, "Go see Tootsie at the Spanish Keys apartments tomorrow. You'll need to check out of the hotel on Friday prior to our flight to New York, and I've arranged for you to have an apartment there. After practice tonight, go by and introduce yourself to Joe Campisi. He owns a good restaurant nearby. It'll be crowded. That's a good sign, right? Tell them Joe's expecting you, and they'll bring you in the back way. He'll be happy to meet you."

Gil's word was good as gold. I met Tootsie at the Spanish

Keys and rented a furnished apartment that overlooked the pool. My new address was 5210 Sandhurst Lane. And the dinner that night at Campisi's was over the top. The place was packed, as Gil had predicted, customers standing in a line around the block. I shimmied my way through to the back door and told the bouncer there who I was and that Joe was expecting me.

Joe came out, greeted me personally, and escorted me to a small office in the back, where he offered me a seat in a red leather armchair. We talked football for almost an hour. When I was hungry, he escorted me to a private room.

Joe started me out with some of his specialties, including pizza, sautéed crab claws, and garlic butter steak. *I might even begin to gain some weight if I keep eating like this*, I thought. *Not a bad gig, being a Dallas Cowboy.* I'd never eaten that much food, even at Thanksgiving. I could hardly move when I got up to leave.

I thanked Joe, and he gave me a hug.

"Come back often, Robert, my friend. We'll look forward to seeing you soon."

By the end of the season, Joe must have come to regret his offer. I ate there once a week, never paying a penny—despite my repeated entreaties to Joe—for the best meals in Dallas.

Welcome to the NFL

That first week of preparation flashed by. Flying to New York on my first team charter, staying at the ritzy Essex House on Central Park—strange and wonderful experiences. The flight attendants on our charter were all pretty ladies, very accommodating to the Cowboys players and coaches. Coach Landry's control of the team extended to minding our manners, though, and the players all flirted with flight attendants but that was about it.

In New York, we were escorted to the hotel by policemen on motorcycles. The hotel was packed with fans. I couldn't believe my eyes and ears. Fans knew every player by sight and screamed their names as they walked off the team bus. I got off right behind Hollywood Henderson, who flashed his big grin and said to no one in particular, "I have arrived, New York. I have arrived."

The fans ate it up. The players were appreciative of the attention, for the most part, but I could tell that some of them just tolerated it. After that first experience in the spotlight (and not a single fan knew me or my name), I've always thought that living in that kind of a fishbowl 24/7 for a superstar—now, we would think of LeBron James or Tom Brady, who are rarely away from the spotlight—requires a conscious shift in lifestyle. The perks are great, sure, but the attention ruins more careers than it builds.

We were free to eat our Saturday evening meal on our own, as long as we were back at the hotel by eleven o'clock. I was in two hours early, having eaten by myself at a restaurant near the hotel. Anonymous when I wasn't with the team, I could come and go as I pleased. That was nice. But when I stepped into the hotel with the rest of the team, fans asked for autographs.

I had been asked for my autograph in training camp and had refused to sign any because I wasn't a member of the team. Now that I was a Dallas Cowboy, I felt great signing that first program. I wrote my name as perfectly as I had ever written it.

Since I hadn't been asked for my signature a thousand times, I hadn't perfected the scrawl that everyone else had. Most of the players just drew lines, not caring what the result looked like.

I asked Randy Hughes about that. With his usual directness he said, "Don't worry about it, Steele. They don't really want our autographs. They want Staubach, Dorsett, guys like that." I got a chuckle out of that.

"Get used to it, though," he continued, elbowing me in the ribs. "It'll be like this as long as you're a part of the team. These fans are relentless."

So "Steele here" was signing autographs—whether fans wanted it or not—and about to play his first game against the New York Giants in the Meadowlands. I was starting on the kickoff coverage team, second from the right as we ran like hell downfield and tried to make a tackle (and to avoid getting clocked by a bunch of guys equally determined not to let us get in on the action). I knew I probably wouldn't play as a receiver because I was new to the team and better suited to contribute on special teams.

The pregame meal was similar to what I experienced in college: bacon, eggs, and pancakes, with no butter or milk products. Coach Landry made a few statements about getting our heads right for the task at hand, and we boarded the team bus to the stadium.

Again, the fans were everywhere, yelling and screaming every name on the roster.

It was good to be a rookie. A real treat to be a part of the team, the fanfare, the world of pro football—and the reigning World Champions.

Pregame preparation was a blur. I could hear all the rumbling going on, PA announcers giving game notes and starting lineups, some guys going over their assignments one last time, some just finding a zone and visualizing the controlled chaos that was about to explode on the field. Not much different, really, from any college game I had prepared for. Here, though, I wasn't one of the starters, but a member of the supporting cast willing to contribute in any way I could.

Coach Ditka came over and started explaining what I was about to experience. He was the perfect guy to coach special teams, fearless and more than a little bit crazy, and his manic energy rubbed off on me. I couldn't wait to get on the field and show the Cowboys that they had made the right decision by giving me a roster spot.

The Giants won the toss, and I did a couple of jumping jacks to get the blood flowing. Ditka drilled me on staying in my lane, making sure that the ball carrier didn't break containment and get past us. His was the only voice I could hear through the crowd's roar.

We lined up, the referee blew the whistle, and I raced down the field after Rafael Septien's kick.

The Giants' runner caught the ball and came my way as the blockers built their wedge. The biggest of the four looked me square in the eye and shouted to his teammate, "I have him high. You take him low."

You might think that two guys running at you full speed with their intent on destroying you would be intimidating, right?

You are 100 percent correct!

I was petrified. And in that instant, both players hit me with such force—high by the linebacker and low by a backup running back—that I thought my knees were being separated from the rest of my body. The only good thing that happened was I actually took out two of their wedge blockers and allowed some of my teammates to make the tackle at the thirty-five-yard-line.

I limped off the field trying hard not to appear too shaken. Bruce Huther caught my eye and grinned. "Welcome to the NFL," he said, giving me a reassuring pat on the shoulder.

I sat on the bench for a moment, gathered my thoughts, and took inventory to make sure I still had all of my necessary body parts.

Ditka came over and asked me if I was all right. I wasn't sure if I should be concerned—Ditka wasn't the most warm and fuzzy guy you'd ever meet, and I thought maybe he saw the hit and got worried for my well-being—but then I realized that he was just checking in. When he left to talk to the other guys on the kickoff squad, I thought, *I'm game for this, even if it kills me.*

We won the game 34–24. The media came around and asked questions of many of the team's stars. One reporter asked me what it was like to play in my first pro game.

"I'm just glad to be a part of the team. It was a good win," I told him. He shook his head politely, but it wasn't really what he was looking for, so I'm sure it was never printed.

The plane ride home wasn't like any bus trip back to Florence, Alabama, but more like a fraternity party—plenty of beer and a jubilant mood all around. Since I was new, I just sat in my seat and tried to blend in. Some of the guys were having way too much fun, and the first class cabin was blocked off. Coach Landry and his staff were up there minding their own business, holding court with the media that moved back and forth through the curtain that separated first class and coach and already game-planning Week 3 against the Los Angeles Rams.

We were 2–0 and headed toward another bright Super Bowl season. I remember that next week really starting to pay attention to what Coach Landry had to say to us in the meetings, because I knew that playing under his leadership was an honor I would value the rest of my life.

"We've got to start strong and finish strong. Remember, we'll hit a lull in the middle of the season. It always happens," he told us. "Getting back to the Super Bowl isn't going to be as easy as you guys have made it seem in the first two weeks."

Smiles all around on that one. Coach was conceding that the team was very good—maybe even great—but he wasn't ready to crown us repeat champs yet.

"Every team is gunning for the Dallas Cowboys." That turned out to be his mantra for the season—and it was certainly appropriate.

Every eye in that room was on Coach Landry. Every ear took his message to heart. I've never seen anyone command a room the way Coach did. Without raising his voice, he had the respect of forty-five men who made it their mission to play football at the highest level.

And we were determined to make that hard work pay off in another Super Bowl victory.

The Fabulous Five

Five rookies made the team that summer: four draft choices and one free agent. Statistically speaking, that's 33 percent of the draft choices and 1 percent of the free agents. Alois Blackwell, Tom Randall, Dennis Thurman, and top pick Larry Bethea were the draftees. I was the only free agent out of seventy-nine other Cowboys wannabees.

One day after the Giants game, I found a copy of the previous week's *Cowboys Weekly* near my locker and read about the draft choices who had made the roster. The article talked about how hard a road it was and went into great detail about the accomplishments of "the four who made it."

I reread the article several times, because I knew that the writer had made a mistake—even though the piece had been published before I joined the team. It should have read "the five who made it." *Cowboys Weekly* ran another article later that month correcting the oversight and introducing all of the rookies in more detail.

While "the five" had finally made the team, we were still unproven rookies. Coach Landry didn't play rookies except on special teams or in circumstances when a starter—a veteran—got hurt, which was always a possibility in the bruising world of pro football. He didn't see any of us as seasoned enough, tested by fire, or capable of being depended upon fully. Time was a rookie's best friend and his worst enemy. The longer you stayed around, the more coaches and your teammates warmed up to you. A rookie needed to produce when he had a chance, though, or he wouldn't be around for long.

Each of the "fabulous five," as we came to be known, contributed on special teams, with Dennis Thurman having the biggest overall impact. The team had chosen Dennis Thurman in the eleventh round, and he knew from the outset that to play, he would have to pay his dues on special teams. He wasn't going to replace Charlie Waters or Cliff Harris overnight, but he would be prepared just in case.

Dennis was a smart, talented player who had what it took to get along with his teammates. I could see Dennis becoming a key part of the secondary. All of us just needed some time under our belts to learn the system and get game experience before we would be trusted on the field full-time.

I looked forward to the challenge.

Spalding Pyron

My college fraternity brother and best friend, Spalding Pyron, visited me in Dallas after I made the team. He loved the place from the day he got there and decided he would relocate, moving with me into my two-bedroom apartment. Spalding often made spur-of-the-moment decisions, but this was a big one even for him. I didn't balk at the idea, since it would save me money. I certainly didn't have time during the season to meet anyone else around town. We had always gotten along well, even though we had never roomed together in college.

During college, we would take spontaneous trips now and then. Spalding's dad had a 1976 GMC motor home, and in 1978, we took a trip to the hills of North Carolina to go snow skiing. I was in the middle of my senior year of college, having finished my last season of football at UNA and planning on heading into the business world.

We were in Boone, North Carolina, on Sunday, January 15, 1978, when Super Bowl XII was played in New Orleans. I watched the game on and off and remember seeing Butch Johnson's tremendous touchdown catch in the Cowboys' victory, but Spalding and I weren't that focused on the game. Other than knowing the Cowboys as "America's Team," I didn't know any of the players, nor did I really know who Tom Landry was, except for his trademark hat and his reputation as a stand-up guy.

Nine months later, I was playing for the Cowboys, and my friend Spalding had made himself at home. He didn't waste any time blending into the Dallas singles environment. Within a couple of weeks of arriving, he got a job at a local camera shop and began dating several ladies from Southern Methodist University. He and I ended up spending little time together because our lives were beginning to move fast in different directions. I had a job that required studying at night and a regular practice schedule, as well as long stretches away from the apartment. But we enjoyed hanging out with each other when we could, and it sure was nice to have a friendly face around in the high-pressure atmosphere of that first year. Spalding would have never moved to Dallas had it not been for me, and he still lives there. I was the best man in his wedding, and he was the best man in mine.

We would often laugh about the Boone trip and reminisce about watching the game at a distance, never imagining that less than a year later we would be in Dallas together and a part of that scene.

Home Opener, Texas Stadium

We traveled to the infamous Los Angeles Coliseum to play the Los Angeles Rams and suffered our first loss of the season, my first taste of defeat as a Cowboy. The flight home was quite a bit different from the raucous ride back from the Week 2 victory at the Meadowlands. No one talked. Guys just sat in their seats nursing injuries with ice packs, taking beers from the flight attendants and thinking about how we were going to recover from the loss. Getting our lunch handed to us this early in the season—the final score was 27–14, but the newspaper accounts suggested that the game wasn't even that close—gave me a glimpse into how Coach Landry handled the team after a defeat.

Practice that week in preparation for a home game against the Saint Louis Cardinals was business as usual. Coach Landry's expression didn't change much, which I found comforting. But you could hear a pin drop when we gathered on Monday at 10:00 a.m., the day after the Rams' win, to review game films.

No one had to tell us, but the evidence was right there in front of us. We had played poorly, turning the ball over five times. The running game was held to ninety-six yards, and the Rams never let up, instead kicking us around as if to prove that Dallas could be had just like every other team in the league.

The NFL has never been a league where a team can rest on its laurels. The surest sign of a coming loss is for a team to start to believe its own press clippings.

During the film review, Coach Landry would make comments about particular plays, sometimes showing a play again and again to drive home a point. The offending player would bury his head in his hands as if it would make the play somehow go away before Coach Landry could queue it up again and show us the ugly truth. Coach never berated players verbally, letting the film speak for itself.

The old saying is never more true than in an NFL prep meeting: "The big eye in the sky don't lie."

The cameras caught every move of every player on every play. Today, I shudder when I think of how much more effective teams have gotten at tracking players; one need only watch a game on television to realize how absurd it is for a player to think that he can get away with *anything* on the field.

After a solid week of practice and preparation, I was ready for my first home game against Saint Louis. I was comfortable back in the stadium where I had played a couple of preseason games. As a full-fledged member of the team, I embraced the crowd and was ready for a great game.

We didn't disappoint, playing with more focus and more energy than the week before. Despite turning the ball over twice, our offense got back on track and the defense played with the kind of passion that made Coach Landry proud. I know I had a blast chasing punts downfield and covering kickoffs.

When I wasn't on the field, I got caught up in the emotion of the game and the crowd just like everyone else. That day was my first time watching Crazy Ray, up close and personal. Crazy Ray (his real name was Wilford Jones) was a character, a black man dressed in a cowboy suit who would whistle and holler from the sidelines. Ray started his career with the Cowboys as a souvenir salesman during the team's infancy before becoming an icon for his cheerleading and presence during the games. Between 1962 and his death in 2007—forty-six seasons in all—he missed three home games.

Crazy Ray was as entertaining as the famous cheerleaders, and his legacy has been passed down from generation to generation.

Red Zone Rules

Thank Your Lucky Stars

"People look at the score and assume they know what happened, but winning and losing sometimes isn't just about who puts more points on the board. If you've got a never-say-die attitude and you continue to work hard, then you may not be successful at football, but you're going to be successful at something," says Dan Reeves.

"In a team sport, wins and losses are about getting people to play together unselfishly. What you have to do is give everything you've got to make the people around you better."

Relish that special moment you've worked hard to reach. When you dare to dream big, the moment will come.

Enjoy it.

And always show your appreciation. Be thankful for what you've accomplished, for the place you've reached, and for everyone who helped you along the way. Whatever your goals may be, you make it happen, but it's a team effort. Others have a hand in helping you get there. Remember to appreciate them. Thank them whenever possible.

Reaching your dream, or even pursuing it, will bring new experiences your way. Enjoy the whole experience, the newness of it all, the excitement.

You've earned it!

And remember, even if the only shot you have is a million-to-one, take it. That one-in-a-million shot is your "in." Make the most of it.

As we always used to say when we ran out onto the field at Texas Stadium and looked toward mid-field and its unmistakable logo, "Thank your lucky stars!"

Be a Real Pro

"I never lost sight of having fun. I never lost sight that I was actually living a dream," says Charlie Waters. "I'm so very thankful that I got to experience the NFL. My greatest moment as a player was a nothing moment. It was on the sidelines at the 1977 Super Bowl, the year before Robert came in.

"Our whole defensive team had a great game. I didn't do anything special in the game. I made some plays, but I remember when that game was over and I looked around at my buddy Cliff Harris. He and I came in together. We were two young kids just out of college, same age, playing safety. We played together the whole time we were in Dallas. We made eye contact with each other and we just kind of nodded our heads. You know, 'This is a job well done.'

"And that moment had great significance for both of us. Landry used to hold people in high regard if you could really call them 'pro.' If you held the status of a pro, you were a made man. I heard him say on a few occasions how difficult it was to become a pro, a person who knows how to win.

"Any competitor is motivated after a loss, because they've got something to prove. Watching how a guy responds when he wins, though, is a true test of character. Can he win again? And we won in 1971, when Cliff and I were first coming up. We came back—it took us five years or six, but we came back—and we won again. To me, that was the epitome. Everybody's gunning for you and you've got confidence. If you can learn how to win again after you've already won, then you've accomplished something.

"That was my greatest moment as an athlete."

A Cowboy's Lifestyle

Dressing for Success

When I left my parents' house in a rush on the way back to Dallas after Gil Brandt's call, I told myself I would just buy what I needed when I got there. The team was headed to Washington on Saturday morning for a Sunday tilt with the Redskins. I planned to have dinner Saturday night at a fancy restaurant with Jackie, my new lady friend.

Jackie, the Braniff flight attendant for the team's charter, was a beautiful, stylish woman in her early thirties. I valued Jackie's advice, so when she told me—kindly but firmly—that I needed to spruce up my wardrobe, I took her advice seriously. I knew for certain that when it came to clothing, she had the edge on me. I was so concerned about making the team, I never had the time or the desire to dress in anything but sweats and jeans.

If I wanted to spend time with Jackie, that was going to change.

We got in her car one afternoon and headed to a local shopping district. She gave me a purposeful up-and-down and said, "Yes, sir, we really need to upgrade your wardrobe."

The "we" in her sentence was a direct message: *You still look like an immature college boy. I'm trying to help you out here in the real world.*

I offered the best excuses I had, only a couple legitimate. "You don't understand. I may be a Cowboy, but I don't make a lot of money. I don't really like shopping. . . ."

When that didn't work, I tried the lamest of them all: "I don't even know where to go."

"We'll figure that out, rookie." She took me to a few classic men's clothing stores where thousand-dollar suits hung on the rack out front (no telling what they had back in the limited-access area). I squeamishly picked out a blue blazer and a pair of khaki dress slacks, two shirts, and a couple of ties. The modest haul took most of my first month's paycheck—almost more than I had paid for my first car.

Despite my unease at spending that kind of money on clothes, Jackie was right. NFL players were supposed to look the part and dress appropriately. We all wore coats and ties on road trips, and I didn't know how other players managed—until I discovered their secret: Woody Stogo's.

Jackie wanted me to buy a lot more clothes since we were going out on the town on the nights she wasn't flying. On my salary, in the places she wanted to take me, that would have been impossible. I asked my teammates in the locker room if anyone knew of deals on nice clothes. Randy Hughes, one of the best-dressed guys on the team, told me about Woody Stogo's, a well-guarded secret at the Dallas Apparel Mart.

Stogo's carried suits, jackets, and trousers—the essentials—and a good suit, which might have been $1,000 (about $3,000 today) in a retail store was $200 at Stogo's. After buying a suit, two sport coats, and five pair of pants—and breathing a sigh of relief that I was going to be able to cover my rent—I was decked out.

We went to Washington that weekend and lost 9–5 in a game featuring two stout defenses feeling each other out for a meeting later in the season. More baseball than football, a score like that, but the Redskins had gotten the best of us. Five games into the season, the World Champion Cowboys were a mediocre 3–2. A long way from where we thought we would be, for sure, but every team wanted to take us out, as Coach Landry reminded us. Every play was a battle. Our Flex defense was playing well, but the offense hadn't gelled well enough that we should have been considered NFC favorites, let alone Super Bowl contenders.

Coach Landry was in a particularly bad mood for the film sessions when we got back to Dallas. Being the consummate professional, though, he kept his comments focused on what we did well (not so much) and what we needed to do better (just about everything). We knew we had a lot of work ahead of us, and even the veterans, stung by an inauspicious start to the season, looked forward to getting back out on the practice field.

Those first few weeks were difficult, but not so much for what happened on the field. After all, I had been through the crucible, and I felt comfortable on the football field. No, the real adjustment came in learning how to handle myself off the field, particularly how I presented myself in public (Jackie's suggestion that I "update my wardrobe" was a big step) and how I dealt with the media.

Several weeks after the Washington game, a reporter interviewed me about my life with the Cowboys for a piece in a Dallas newspaper. He started with what I thought was a harmless enough question.

"Robert, you're new to Dallas. Probably quite a bit different from Columbus, Georgia. What's been your biggest adjustment so far?"

Boy, did I have a ready answer for that one.

"Wearing a coat and tie on the road," I told him without hesitating. The answer got a laugh. "And trying to keep up with the more fashion-conscious players on the team. Those guys all make more money than I do."

"You look sharp. Where are you buying your clothes?"

"I've really enjoyed getting to know Dallas. I got most of my new clothes from Woody Stogo at the Apparel Mart."

The comment made the Dallas newspaper—and not in a good way. Stogo's personnel must have been cursing me when the phone started to ring with Dallas-area men asking for the same discount the Cowboys got.

I had only been interviewed a few times in my life by my hometown or university newspapers. When a reporter asked me questions, I told the truth. Simple enough. But I didn't know the media played games, trying to catch players off guard and looking for story lines. After all, an honest question deserved an honest answer.

I soon discovered how wrong I was.

Gil Brandt phoned me the next morning and let me know my comments—in fact, any players' comments to the media—represented the whole organization. He wasn't asking me to lie or even make things up, just informing me that I should carefully consider each question and respond only when comfortable that my answers would represent the best interests of the Dallas Cowboys. He told me that my comments about Woody Stogo would probably cost the players their access to the apparel mart (or, at the very least, Woody's), something I'd have to answer for in the locker room.

I explained to Gil that I didn't know I had made a mistake. I bought some clothes, paid with a check, and had no knowledge that I had done anything inappropriate. It seemed as retail to me as any store I'd shopped in before.

Boy, was I wrong.

The next morning, the players gave me a hard time at first and then relented, telling me about their first experiences with being misquoted, misunderstood, and misrepresented by an inquisitive media. When I started paying more attention to how they responded to questions in postgame interviews, I heard hesitation in their voices as they gave guarded responses without much substance (when I turn on the television today, I understand how far players have come in that regard, learning from early in their careers that any provocative answer will bounce around the 24/7 echo chamber until it drives everybody crazy and makes a lot of people look bad).

The media simply looked for anything to print, and many reporters tried to make a name for themselves on the way up in their respective careers. So I made the interviews a game.

Keep your eyes open and your mouth shut. Watch the other players and learn from them, not just on the football field but off as well. I could hear Harlon Hill's voice in my head. I've never gotten better advice.

In the case of my gaffe with the Stogo's comment, the media had a field day, writing about special privileges for players that others didn't get. What did I know? I thought everyone had access to the Apparel Mart. Obviously, only retail stores and apparel-industry insiders had that sort of access. So I was blowing the lid off a perk, and I paid the price (so to speak). I never went back to Stogo's, though I'm sure Woody kept granting access as long as he didn't receive any more unwanted recognition.

In the end, it was an eye-opening experience, a lesson learned without too much damage done.

This is the big leagues, rookie. You'll do better from now on when speaking to the media.

Saint Louis Special Teams

We were getting ready to play the Saint Louis Cardinals when I got a nice surprise phone call from my sister Vicki. She called to tell me she and her husband, Hugh, were going to be in town for a business meeting and asked if I would like to have dinner with them. We set a time, and I was checking into my room when Rafael Septien asked me if I would like to go see the Gateway Arch with him. I'd never been to Saint Louis, so I told him I would tag along. I certainly had no interest in staying in my hotel room. I'd prepared for the game as well as I could. As in school, there comes a time when you know the material cold and any more studying would be overload.

Rafael and I grabbed a cab and headed to the arch. From the bottom, it's quite an impressive structure, the tallest monument in America at 630 feet. Until we got there, I didn't know that the elevator at the bottom of the arch actually took passengers *through* the arch. Rafael and I climbed into the tight little seats (he had a better time of it, since he was about a foot shorter than I was). My knees were in my chin, and Rafael reclined like he was sitting in a lounge chair.

It was good seeing my sister again. She and Hugh have great friends they were having dinner with, and I laughed most of the evening. Hugh worked for Tom's Foods, the snack food company headquartered in our hometown. Hugh was a marketing vice president and provided me with "samples."

I became a much more popular player on the team once I started receiving my Tom's samples of snacks, crackers, cookies, and potato chips. I ate all my favorites, and I had plenty of teammates stopping by my locker to see what I had left over. When I mentioned to my brother-in-law how much I missed my Tom's snacks—Dallas was the international headquarters for their nemesis, Lay's Potato Chips, so Tom's had been crowded out of the market—Hugh promised to send samples to Dallas so I could share the product with my newfound teammates. Introducing them to Tom's Foods seemed like a great idea to me.

The Saint Louis trip was the most memorable in my career to that point. We won the game, and I put a memorable lick on a wedge blocker on the kickoff. The ball carrier had taken an initial hit and was fighting for extra yards. I was about to hit the pile when one of their receivers stepped in front of me. I hit him at full stride, knocking him over the pile. He rolled to a stop three or four yards on the other side of the pile and lay there for a second, face down.

I had hit him so hard, I thought he might get up and want to fight. But he turned over on his back, got his feet under him, and without batting an eye, he looked at me and said, "Great hit, eighty-one. See you later." He patted me on the butt and ran off the field.

I jogged off in amazement, not sure if he got hit like that a lot and wasn't all there or if he, like me, was a special teams junky and enjoyed delivering—and taking, if necessary—honest, hard hits. ("When it comes to special teams," Ditka would snarl, " 'tis always better to give than to receive.")

Either way, I was still shaking my head when I ran back to chase the next kickoff. The guy I had blocked earlier was smart to react the way he did, because my head was on a swivel. I didn't want to take a shot from the blind side to make up for the one I had given him. I made it through the game unscathed, and after a 21–12 win, the plane ride home was a little rambunctious, a bunch of guys telling all their game stories about great hits, great plays, and keeping their quarterback, Jim Hart, on his back most of the day.

Running around the back of the plane with Jackie and her flight attendant coworkers was a treat, too. Jackie always pulled out a bottle of wine or two for me as a parting gift. Another perk for being on America's Team.

Something for the pain? Try this.

You think acupuncture might work? We've got that covered.

This was the locker room of the World Champion Dallas Cowboys, and we were treated like champions.

I remember walking in from practice after suffering from the flu. Coach Landry met me at the entrance to the practice field and asked me how I was doing. One of the players waited for me after Landry walked away.

"Is that what it takes to get Landry to speak with you, recovering from the flu?"

Coach didn't speak to many players in the locker room.

My locker was between Larry Cole and Rayfield Wright, two of the biggest and longest-tenured guys on the team. Rayfield is in the Hall of Fame and Larry deserves to be there. I tried to keep out of their way as much as possible, but sometimes Larry's stuff spilled over into my locker area. He wasn't the world's neatest person. But when it came to performing on the field, few were better or went about the job with a simpler, more honest approach.

Most players had fifteen or twenty pairs of shoes in their locker for different field surfaces. Larry had two pairs (which always made me wonder where all that junk came from). He didn't make a fuss about much, just went about his business, playing football and delivering for his team without ever seeking recognition.

There were other special moments, but sharing would break the locker room mentality. I won't do that.

To this day, I respect the code.

Red Zone Rules

Right Place, Right Time

"My best memory of Robert was as this tall, lanky guy with a tremendous attitude," says Roger Staubach.

"Didn't hurt that he was a big target. For a quarterback, he was the kind of receiver you like to throw the ball to.

"For him to make the team was a fantastic success. Robert was there at a very good time for the Cowboys."

Image Is Everything

When you're striving for success, especially when your job requires you to be in the public eye, you need to look like you belong.

Dress for success, right?

I didn't much care for shopping, but when my trusted friend told me I needed to update my wardrobe, I listened.

Set aside some funds to invest in your image.

Once you've got the image down, learn how to talk with the media. When you're a novice, they'll catch you off guard and often use your words against you or your team. It's their job—the more sensational a piece, the more readers or viewers they attract.

Brace yourself. Don't be dishonest, but don't feel that you have to reveal everything. Watch your words.

And think before you speak. Or as the old adage goes, "Better to keep your mouth shut and let people think you're a fool than to open your mouth and remove all doubt."

Play Solitaire

"We used to have this rule that until the rookies made the team and were on the team for at least three games, only then we would start learning first names," says Charlie Waters.

"No sense in becoming good friends with a guy who's gone the next day. It's a rough business. And I really liked Robert.

"I saw myself in him. . . . But we refused to make it personal."

12

Thanksgiving

More Media

Before the 1978 Thanksgiving Day game against the Washington Redskins, a famous broadcaster came up and introduced himself to me.

"Robert, how you doing? Just wanted to check in. Now that you have a few games in the NFL under your belt, tell me what it's like playing for the Cowboys."

"Having the time of my life," I told him, staying jovial but keeping my comments as neutral as I could after my earlier foot-in-mouth experience. "Can't think of anything else I'd rather be doing."

"You're a long way from UNA, aren't you?"

"Sure. But the field at UNA is a hundred yards long and the object of the game hasn't changed," I joked.

He chuckled about that. Such a simple view of the game must have sounded naïve to a guy who had interviewed every great player in the last two decades.

"But aren't you disappointed that you haven't made a catch

this year? Word from the front office is that you've got the best hands on the team."

I decided to play it safe. The reporter was a real pro at earning players' confidence and drawing them out while getting them to say what he wanted to hear.

"I don't know anything about that, sir. I do know that I enjoy being here, and I'll do whatever the team asks me to do. I understand the system and the philosophy, and I'm working hard to prove my worth to the team. If somebody gets hurt, I'm ready to play. And if they throw me the ball, I'll plan on catching it."

I thought I had handled the situation well, but what the broadcaster said next caught me off guard.

"You don't understand, Robert. There are people in the game—people whose opinion I respect a great deal—who have told me in confidence that you could start for *any* other NFL team. But you seem to be happy sitting on the bench here and not getting a pass thrown your way. If you have the best hands on the team, why aren't they throwing to you?"

He was pushing it. What did he want?

I stuck with the party line. "Look, I'm really happy to be here, just to be a part of this team and its great tradition. And I'll do whatever it takes to continue to be a part of this team. If that means catching a pass or blocking a punt, then that's what I'll do."

He pushed a little more, and I was brusque.

"Sir, I've got to get prepared for a ballgame."

The man never said another word to me, but the comments made the rounds about my having the best hands on the team. The nickname "Flypaper" stuck.

Thanksgiving Day "Hit"

Playing the Washington Redskins on national television on Thanksgiving Day was a special treat. Having gotten embarrassed in DC earlier in the season, we weren't about to let that happen again—especially at home.

We beat the Redskins 37–10 and dominated every phase of the game. In fact, it was one of the few games during the 1978 season that I had a chance to play wide receiver. With a big lead early, the coaches shut the passing game down. Instead, we focused on running the ball, killing the clock, and adding another one to the *W* column without risking injury to our star players.

There was little chance that any passes were going to be thrown my way, but I ran my routes and blocked as if the game was on the line. Live-game experience was hard for a reserve to come by on the Cowboys, and I wanted to make the most of it. One of the defensive players, Mike Hegman, came up to me on the sideline and told me to take it easy, to save myself.

But the struggle I had gone through to get to that field had made taking plays off impossible. I recalled a time or two early in the second half when Coach Landry looked on in a silent rage on the sideline as our superstar running back Tony Dorsett would break a tackle at the line of scrimmage and then get taken down in the open field by a defensive back who should have been blocked by a receiver—and the receiver was standing fifteen yards from the play watching the whole thing develop like he was at a bar checking out the game on television.

Just because we had the game in hand didn't mean that we shouldn't continue to work on the fundamentals. And I certainly didn't want to be on the receiving end of a game-film tirade from Ditka, who was at least as scary in the darkness of the film room as he was on the practice field or the sideline when he lost his mind over a missed assignment.

So I kept running and blocking harder than ever.

We scored another touchdown, taking advantage of a depleted Washington defense, and I was on the kick-coverage team. Running downfield as hard as I could, I took a hit that I never saw coming. One second, I was flying down the hash mark near the middle of the field. The next, I was lying at Coach Landry's feet. When I came to, Ditka was standing over me.

"You OK, rookie? You gonna live?" There was a little concern in his voice—or what passed for concern with him—but he was looking at me like something he had just scraped off his shoe.

Everything hurt three different ways, and I had the irresistible urge to just close my eyes and take a nap right there on the Astroturf, in front of seventy-five thousand fans.

I tried to nod my head inside the helmet. All Ditka could see was my chin moving up and down a couple of inches. That was enough for him. My neck wasn't broken—even if every little movement was deliberate and painful—so how bad could it be?

Ditka shook his head and wandered away to check in with the rest of the special teams players.

After the game, Hegman approached me and gave me a pitying look.

"I told you to slow down, Steele. The other guys knew enough to slow down. And you went out there and got hammered."

He started to walk away and then turned back.

"It's a long season, rookie. Save yourself, and you'll be useful to the team when we need you. Next time we're up four touchdowns on a team, remember that."

#82

Our tight end, Jay Saldi, broke his hand during a game, and by Monday morning, with Jay in a cast up to his elbow, Ditka came by my locker and asked me if I would play tight end.

"I'll play any position, Coach," I told him. Of course, I was talking to a guy who had been inducted into the Hall of Fame at the position, so I wondered how much faith he had in my ability to line up at tight end. "I haven't practiced at the position, but I could learn the plays."

Anything to get on the field. Anything to keep myself on this team.

At six foot four and 198 pounds with a body-fat reading of 1.9 percent, I wouldn't be the most imposing tight end in the NFL. But I would sure as hell give it a shot.

Ditka thanked me when I told him I'd be happy to take on the challenge. The next day, he came back to my locker with a serious look—not unusual for him.

"I've got some good news."

"Great, Coach. What's that?"

"We've picked up Jackie Smith out of retirement. We talked him into taking Jay Saldi's spot for the rest of the season."

"I guess that is good news," I told Ditka. I didn't know why he was sharing that with me, but it sounded like I was losing the back-up position at tight end before I ever played a down.

"Jackie's one of the best tight ends ever. Played nineteen seasons for the Saint Louis Cardinals. He'll go into the Hall of Fame when he hangs 'em up." High praise, coming from Ditka. He stood in front of me, kind of shifting his weight from one foot to the other and wringing his hands. Very unlike Ditka to show any sort of nervousness, particularly around players, where his word was gospel.

"I need to say this, Robert. You know the Cowboys have always respected people's numbers. If you're number eighty-one, you'll be eighty-one as long as you want it."

"Mike, I really have no clue where this conversation is going."

"Jackie wore eighty-one with the Cardinals his whole career."

"Ah. . . ." The light bulb went on. I could keep my jersey number, no questions asked. But when word got back to the veterans that a rookie had denied a Hall of Famer the chance to play one last season with his old number, I would lose a lot of credibility with the guys.

"Like I said, you're eighty-one as long as you want to be," Ditka continued. He was pressing, and I can't say that I didn't enjoy the feeling of making him sweat for a minute or two.

Finally, I let him off the hook.

"Coach, as long as I have a number in my locker today for practice, I don't care if it's eighty-one or eight hundred eighty-one. I just want a number."

"Great. Coach Landry thought you'd have that attitude, and I appreciate it. Makes things a lot easier."

It really wasn't a big deal to me, and I was naïve about most pro football traditions, so I just gave up the #81. From then to the end of my brief career as a Dallas Cowboy, I would be #82.

In football lore, players are adamant about keeping their numbers. In today's NFL, players sell numbers to other players for unreasonable sums of money (in 2004, Washington Redskins defensive back Ifeanyi Ohalete sold his #26 to teammate Clinton Portis for a reported $40,000—quite a bit more than my salary for the 1978 season).

And in hindsight, after I had taken #82, I wish I never had. I should have asked for #29, my number in training camp. That should have been my number to begin with. That was the number I played the preseason in and made the team with.

Thanksgiving at Staubach's

I had a feeling that Thanksgiving was going to be special. We had beaten the Redskins soundly on Thursday, and the team celebrated Thanksgiving and the big win on Friday.

After the game, Coach Jim Myers, who hadn't said three words to me all season, asked me what my plans were.

"Nothing special," I said, expecting him to wish me a happy holiday before leaving for a much-needed break. Our next game would be in eleven days against the New England Patriots—not the toughest game we'd play all year, but one we had to win to set ourselves up for a play-off run. Instead, Myers invited me to Roger Staubach's house to celebrate Thanksgiving with his family.

I was flattered by the invitation but wondered why Roger hadn't asked me himself.

I figured it out when I heard the punch line.

"My niece is in town, and she'd love to be your date for dinner," Coach Myers said. Despite using the back door to spend Thanksgiving at Staubach's, I gladly accepted. I didn't even ask Coach Myers for a description of his niece—oddly, he didn't offer one—an oversight I understood later.

I arrived on time to join a crowd of Cowboys players, coaches, and their families. Roger's wife, Maryanne, was a tremendous hostess. I was impressed with Roger's house—a pool with an automatic cover, a backyard covered entirely in Astroturf. We played basketball and enjoyed the afternoon socializing with the rest of the Dallas Cowboys family.

I know I was chosen to be my date's escort because I was single and available. She was very nice, a good conversationalist—and someone I knew I would never see again. I was a gentleman, stayed an appropriate amount of time, and breathed a sigh of relief when I pulled my car out of the driveway.

Blind dates rarely become love at first glance. Sometimes, even Cupid misses.

Divisional Play-offs: Cowboys vs. Falcons (12/30/78)

Making the divisional play-offs was Coach Landry's first goal, a benchmark he set for the team in training camp in Thousand

Oaks. Of course, going back to the Super Bowl again for a second year was the ultimate goal for the season—and one still within our reach.

We had finished the regular season with a solid 12-4 record and were headed into the play-offs on a six-game winning streak, having run the table after a lackluster loss in Miami at the beginning of November. Tony Dorsett was running to form—he finished the regular season with more than 1,300 yards rushing—and Staubach, at thirty-six a lethal combination of experience and athleticism, was a surgeon on the field, picking apart opposing defenses and exposing weaknesses in ways that had even coaches slack-jawed.

We drew the Atlanta Falcons in the divisional play-offs, and the game was going to be special for me. My parents, grand-parents, and my old roommate Spalding would be there. Growing up in Columbus, the Falcons were the favored team, but one I never followed. I'd never been to a game and couldn't tell you more than three players' names prior to our preparation for the game. Calling it a rivalry would have been an overstatement.

Still, I had never been so ready to play.

The mistake I made, though, was getting a personal foul on the opening kickoff of the second half.

Nothing got Mike Ditka's ire up any faster than a stupid penalty on special teams.

Because he was both receivers coach and special teams coach, I came into contact with Ditka more often than any other coach on the staff. We spent a lot of time together going over kick-coverage schemes and learning the habits of opposing teams, as well as analyzing the key plays and stunts we might pull on kick-off and punt returns.

I gave Ditka full effort on every play and felt like he appreciated my determination on special teams. He knew I was willing to go to the wall for the team and would pay any price, including sacrificing my body for success (something he surely realized after I got my clock cleaned against Washington in the Thanksgiving Day game).

In return, Ditka put his trust in me on special teams.

The one and only time I let Ditka down was in that first play-off game, a close-scoring contest, when I chased the opening kickoff for the second half. The tackle was made on the off-side of the field, and when I started to jog off the field after the play, I realized that the referees had called a personal foul on me.

I trailed the ball carrier, who picked his way up the sideline and was pushed out around the forty. Toward the end of the play, a Falcons linebacker came at me from the blind side and almost took my head off. I went back at him with my arms extended and my hands balled into fists, trying to block him. To the referees, it must have looked like a punch. I was protecting myself, but the linebacker turned to the official standing beside us and begged for a penalty.

The ref obliged.

As so often happens in the controlled chaos that is special teams, the referee calls the wrong player for the penalty. Even though the linebacker attacked me—he played me well, catching me off guard when I should have had my head on a swivel—I was the one who got the penalty. (My cousin, caught for posterity my least proud moment in a Cowboys uniform, snapping a picture of me standing on the sidelines watching the referee walk off the fifteen-yard penalty. To this day, that picture hangs in my home.)

The penalty instantly incurred Ditka's wrath.

When I got to the sideline, Ditka slammed his clipboard down and cussed me up one side and down the other. I was ten feet from him but wishing I were at the South Pole.

Earth, open up now and swallow me. . . .

"Coach, I'm sorry. Nothing happened. The guy begged a call and he got it!" A preemptive strike, before Ditka could start in on me. I knew it sounded lame, but it was all I had.

That just pissed Ditka off even more.

"Come on, Steele. At least take responsibility for what you do on the football field. That's bullshit, and you know it." His shoulders were back, and he jammed his face into mine. He was a master at taking away space from players and making them wither under that maniacal stare.

The penalty gave the Falcons excellent field position on our side of the fifty-yard line. What happened next may have saved my job. Ed "Too-Tall" Jones (who would go on three decades later to star in a Geico commercial, of all things) sacked Steve Bartkowski on three straight plays, pushing the Falcons back deep into their own territory and forcing them to punt.

In the end, we won—barely—27–20. The game could have gone either way, and a loss would have been the worst possible way to end the season. We had entered the game big favorites.

My penalty could have been a significant turning point. Big plays win games, and sometimes big mistakes—like penalties—lose games.

Our defense had done a tremendous job of limiting Bartkowski, Atlanta's talented, mobile, young quarterback, and our offense did enough to win the game, despite Staubach being knocked out of the game with a concussion. His backup, Danny White, a consummate pro who was used to putting out fires when Roger couldn't go, finished the second half. Danny did a great job of running the offense, just as he did every week in practice.

As was his way, Landry had every player prepared in case he was called on to fill in. That preparation was key in helping the team to overcome injuries—an unnerving reality in the NFL and something that all championship teams did well.

I was happy to be moving on to the NFC Championship game in Los Angeles.

NFC Championship Game: Cowboys vs. Rams (01/07/79)

I'd lived in Dallas almost six months and hadn't found the time to buy myself a pair of cowboy boots, something I'd always wanted. In Texas, the boots make the man. I don't know if that's necessarily true, but when in Los Angeles. . . .

The anticipation surrounding our trip to the City of Angels to take on the favored Rams in the NFC Championship game was unlike anything I'd experienced to that point in my career. The team hotel was the Century Plaza in Century City, and, as luck would have it, a specialty shop right down the street sold high-end cowboy boots.

Funny that I ended up buying my cowboy boots not in Dallas but in LA. When my parents asked me why I didn't buy my boots in Texas instead of California—my dad said it was like buying boiled peanuts in Kenosha, Wisconsin, something no one raised in Georgia would even consider—I reminded them that I never had time to shop in Dallas. When we were on the road, we often had a chance to walk around and take in the sights and sounds of a city, one of the things that I enjoyed most about my time in the NFL.

I was surprised that the store carried my size and color preference. Not only did I buy the boots, but I ended up wearing them home from the game after we clinched a spot in the upcoming Super Bowl.

Unlike our earlier meeting in Week 3, when we had turned the ball over five times in a 27–14 loss, the Cowboys had full retribution. This time, the Rams were the team to commit five turnovers, and our defense blanked a potent offense led by quarterback Pat Haden, running back Cullen Bryant, and wide outs Ron Jessie and Willie Miller. The final score was 28–0, though the game was close through the first three quarters (and scoreless at the half), before we scored three touchdowns in the final fifteen minutes.

The NFC Championship was a classic Cowboys win. Great offense, great defense, and a handful of big plays that just broke the opponent's spirit.

After a rough 3-2 start, we were going back to the Super Bowl. We did what we had to do, winning key games—especially those late in the season when we really needed them—and gaining the momentum that all great teams have when they peak at the right time.

We won handily, so the outcome was never really in doubt, but I remember three things about that game: getting to play in the Los Angeles Coliseum, winning, and getting the phone number of a Rams cheerleader who had dated one of the quarterbacks from our training camp. She came up to me after the game and told me she had quit dating her college sweetheart from North Texas State. I told her I was disappointed but would love to get together when I got back to town.

Having my parents at the game was nice and something my dad, especially, enjoyed. He had been offered a contract to play for the Los Angeles Rams in 1952 and had turned down the $6,000 salary because his knees were bad and he knew he couldn't raise a family on that salary, moving across the country when my mother was pregnant. So I think it was a special treat for him to see his son play in a game of that importance (he also experienced another common scene at NFL games in those days when a young boy picked his pocket).

The biggest frustration for me was that I was relieved of my holding duties during the game because of my previous penalty against the Falcons. This was solely Coach Landry's punishment, sending me the message—loud and clear—that lapses of judgment wouldn't be tolerated.

A real slap in the face, because I was *the* holder. I had held for every game, and then, because of one misstep, I was relieved of my duties. The wake-up call worked. Such a penalty is effective in helping a player to keep emotions in check and stay present in each moment of the game. I call it mental toughness. Charlie Waters, who didn't want to hold at all, was told he was going to hold for the conference play-off game and that I could earn my holding duties back for the Super Bowl.

Overall, the penalty didn't affect my playing ability. If anything, I was more vigilant of players who wanted to involve me in another high-low scheme, catching rookies like me off guard. Some teams will go after ill-tempered, naïve, or short-fused players, hoping they can provoke another fifteen-yard penalty. When any player makes a mistake as I did, the event reflects a weak link in the team's chain and broadcasts that weakness to other teams. An overly aggressive team member can cause the entire chain to break, resulting in stupid penalties and—in a worst-case scenario—the loss of a game.

Lesson learned.

I wore my boots home on the plane.

Since I was celebrating a 28–0 shellacking of the Rams, the boots seemed like a fitting tribute to my adoptive hometown. I felt like a real Cowboy and had the boots to prove it—even if they came from a fancy LA boutique.

Red Zone Rules

It's a Dog-Eat-Dog World

"Football is so much different today because of the huge salaries. But in those days with the smaller salaries, you still worried about signing a player who you didn't think had a chance to make it," says Gil Brandt.

"If the player got hurt, the team would be liable for $20,000. For that reason, you didn't want to bring somebody to camp who you didn't think had a chance to make it."

Cracking the Code

"What made the Cowboys 'America's Team'? That's a damn good question. What was the difference? I think it was the amount of time the coaches spent teaching the players to play their position. I went to other teams and it was almost like you're expected to know the position and research the other team instead of learning the subtleties, the ins and outs of a particular position," says Bruce Huther.

"A wide receiver may be different because his routes have to be so crisp and on the money. But you think of defense as a guy bird-dogging the ball. Great defense isn't that simple, though. In the Cowboy's system, every position was well defined, and every player knew what to do under every circumstance.

"I think that probably was the key—at least for the defense— the reason the team had done so well. Because players were coached so well."

Mental Lapse

"I'll say this about Coach Landry, he never ever yelled at us for doing something physically wrong. But he would give us the nastiest look you can imagine if you had a mental lapse," recalls Charlie Waters. "And coming from a guy like Coach, that look was more fearsome than any screaming he could've done.

"We had a defense where I was supposed to take the outside away from a receiver, and someone else would take away the inside—a double team of sorts.

"I was responsible for the outside position, but on this particular route, if I looked into the back field and found out what the back was doing, it would give me a hint as to what the wide receiver had in mind. Not just cold reading, mind you, but tendencies we'd recognized after watching hours of game film. If the back ran an out, then the wide receiver usually ran a go from this formation. If the back blocked, then the wide receiver would run the out.

"That scheme was driven home to me by Coach Landry during the week, and when I saw the dummy squad running that play—with Steele at wide out—I didn't keep my eye on the back and I didn't make the play on the out. Total failure.

"If only I'd paid attention to what Coach Landry taught me. You've got to temper everything, as far as reading tendencies. *You anticipate, you don't guess.* There's a big difference. When I didn't make the play, all Coach Landry did was turn around and look at me—*through* me, more like it—and that just killed me. I never made that mistake again.

"He spoke volumes with his eyes. And you didn't want to get *that look.*"

Choose Your Battles

Always do your best, but remember that nobody else "owns you." Yes, there are times when you will have to make sacrifices—talk to the media, listen to your coach or your boss, heck, even take out the trash when you'd rather be watching a game. Sometimes you just do things you'd rather not do. And you do it because you know it's for the good of the team.

But there are other times when it's more appropriate for you to stand up for yourself. That's personal integrity. Don't let other people own you.

In other words, choose your sacrifices and choose your battles. Some good rules to live by when choosing your battles:

- If something is worth fighting for, trust your intuition and act accordingly. If you feel that you should make the sacrifice, go with your instincts.

- When you don't understand the details of something, ask questions. That's how we learn. Ask for clarification. Don't sit back and keep quiet when you're not sure about something. Politely—but firmly—step up and ask your questions.

- Always remember the importance of mental toughness. Believe it or not, it often can overcome any physical weaknesses. The mental edge is one of your most powerful weapons. Every day, work toward developing that edge.

13

The Super Bowl

The Greatest Show on Turf

In the Cowboys 27–10 win over Denver in Super Bowl XII, 102 million viewers had tuned in—more than for any other televised event in history to that point.

Super Bowl XIII, played on January 21, 1979, in Miami's Orange Bowl, would prove to be an even bigger spectacle, with the game's winner becoming the first NFL franchise to bring home a third Vince Lombardi trophy.

Even during the regular season, professional football is played on a grand stage, so it was no surprise that Super Bowl week in Miami was a fantastic, larger-than-life mosh of media intrusions, players' anxieties, and fans' exhilaration. The world was watching, and for the second consecutive year, the Cowboys were in the most intense spotlight in sport. The intensity and focus on the practice field and in the locker room was unlike anything I had ever witnessed before—and in the run-up to the game, things kept getting more unreal by the day.

Each player was given forty tickets to the Super Bowl. Initially, I couldn't think of that many friends and family who would use my tickets, but they started to disappear quickly when people came out of the woodwork. I gave a few to the veterans who had extended family and had run out of tickets. Of course, my family got as many as they needed. And I gave two to Joe Campisi for his generous free meals that kept me going over a long season. Eventually, though, you realize you can't take care of everybody you know.

One of the more bizarre requests for my tickets came from one of my Cowboys coaches, who must have thought that the rookie couldn't possibly know forty people who would want to see the Super Bowl. He asked me to sell him some of my tickets, at a premium. I was sure the tickets were for him, but he acted like they were for some ticket broker. He said the guy wanted to pay me $250 each for as many tickets as I could spare. I should've just given them to family and friends to hand out, but when my coach was asking, I couldn't say no. So I sold him eight of my tickets. (A few years later in a tax audit, an IRS agent couldn't believe I had actually claimed the money for the tickets as income. "Never heard of that before," he said with an impressed shrug before moving on to other receipts.)

Once the incidentals were out of the way—tickets and the media were just a couple of the distractions we lived with after beating the Rams to earn a spot in the Super Bowl—we arrived in Miami a week before the game.

Media Day was a feeding frenzy for both big and small media outlets, and we were fair game. The players met with the media at the practice facility away from the Orange Bowl, but that didn't stop several hundred cameras and newspaper reporters with pens and pads and cassette recorders at the ready to document every word said about the upcoming game against Pittsburgh—or anything else for that matter. The earlier comment I made about

Woody Stogo's was never far from my mind, so I watched every word I said that week.

The only time we got away from the media, really, was during practice, so I looked forward to getting on the field and getting down to business. We went to the Orange Bowl on Friday morning to do a run-through, a nice departure from the chaos. But the general feeling that week was one of fighting distraction—from the extracurricular activities, from family and friends who had traveled a long way to celebrate the day, and from the hordes of fans who wanted to be a part of football history as they mobbed players every time they stepped out of the hotel, tried to get a bite to eat, or just gathered their thoughts in a quiet corner. I wasn't even a starter, but being part of the Cowboys machine meant that even I garnered the kind of attention usually reserved for superstars (and it still makes me appreciate what high-profile players go through *daily* for years and years).

I was surprised that Coach Landry had invited Woody Hayes as his guest to the Super Bowl. Coach Hayes was as much of a celebrity—if not more—than Coach Landry because of his long, successful tenure as the head coach at college football powerhouse Ohio State. Hayes's career had ended in embarrassment, though, when he was fired after the 1978 season for hitting Clemson linebacker Charlie Bauman on the sideline of the Gator Bowl after Bauman's game-clinching interception. The media had a field day (a cautionary tale, maybe, for any aspiring players and coaches), and Hayes, known for his fiery temper as well as his compassion and his dedication to the game's ideals, was unceremoniously relieved of his position.

On the team bus, Hayes shared Coach Landry's seat at the front. Coach Hayes looked like a whipped little boy, carefully picking his way up the steps and dropping into his seat, shoulders slumped against whatever demons he was fighting. I was impressed that Coach Landry had reached out to a senior colleague, especially given the media attention around the Ohio State fiasco and such a poor outcome for the disgraced coach.

But the more I thought about it, the more it made sense. Coach Landry was saying to the world, "Hey, Woody Hayes was a great coach, and he's still my friend. He's going to be by my side here at the Super Bowl because I support him."

Looking back on a simpler time more than thirty years ago, I wonder how much different the response to Hayes's action would have been today, considering much worse things happen on and off the field in just about every twenty-four-hour news cycle.

Coach Landry displayed the character to stick up for and offer respect to one of his own, a coach who had positively shaped a lot of young men over the decades and still deserved a nation's respect. By inviting Hayes to spend the week with us, Coach Landry was showing compassion in the best way he knew how.

Of course, Coach Landry never showed emotion about anything, so interpret the gesture as you will.

The insider stories were intriguing, but for that golden week leading up to January 21, 1979—Super Bowl XIII—the world's attention was on the Orange Bowl and the matchup between the NFL's two undisputed titans, the Cowboys and the Steelers.

Hundreds of reporters crowded into the hotels and the media rooms. Rafael Septien garnered special attention from Spanish media, radio, and television and participated in several Spanish-language broadcasts. From what I observed, the media wanted to chronicle every player's move every single day—maybe a sign of things to come a couple of decades down the road when it would be possible, for better or worse, to keep track of everyone 24/7.

Even a reporter for the *Ledger Enquirer* from my hometown of Columbus, Georgia, interviewed me. Every time I turned around, he wanted to ask me the same question: "What is your experience like? Did you do anything today that you'd like to talk about?"

Couldn't hear that question without remembering Woody Stogo. Needless to say, I didn't share too much information.

I also did an interview for the *Dallas Morning News*. Obviously, every reporter tried to find a new angle on the often-asked question, "This is your first Super Bowl; what do you think?"

The five of us who were new to the Super Bowl were asked every variation on the theme: how we thought, felt, dressed, ate, prepared.

What's it like being a part of the Super Bowl preparation?

How does it feel to be a Cowboys rookie?

What do you think it's going to be like to play in the Super Bowl?

It was also going to be one of the first times a female reporter had been allowed into our sanctuary, the locker room after the game. The guys had fun with the thought of running around trying to get a shower, get dressed, and get out of there with women in our way. It became just another distraction away from the game preparation, although an entertaining one.

Everyone needed a story, and everyone had deadlines. And in the same way that the questions never changed much—let's face it, the media had pretty much sucked the juice out of every interesting detail six hours into the week and still needed to fill column inches—our responses didn't vary a whole lot.

All of the media hype becomes more humorous when you realize that the Cowboys organization had a standard line. We were coached—and in no uncertain terms, ordered—to go with one of the following responses:

We're here to win a football game.

We're here to take care of business.

It's the same week of preparation whether it's the first game of the season or the last game of the season.

One memorable moment in that avalanche of annoying questions was when my grandmother, Gladys, met Roger Staubach for the first time. He was gracious enough to thank her for the pound cake she had sent him all those months before. We all had a good laugh when he told her he was glad I made the team, because he was hoping he would get another pound cake in the future.

Gladys was the life of the party, high energy, meeting as many players as she could. It was sweet of my grandmother to tell me that one of her friends from church had a "niece" that she would like for me to meet. I had already experienced the Thanksgiving "niece" Coach Myers had set me up with, and I didn't want to go that route again.

I politely declined until she filled in one minor detail: that her friend's niece was a Miami Dolphins cheerleader.

"Gladys," I told her, suddenly interested, "please let your friend know that any night would be a good night for me to meet her niece! Please give me her phone number."

We scheduled dinner for the next evening. I knew I was in for a treat when this gorgeous blonde drove up in a red Corvette with the top down. Gladys beamed when she introduced us, and we rode off into the evening talking about football and Miami Beach.

I quickly found out she knew nothing about football and probably would never be a rocket scientist—but she was definitely one good-looking woman. We ended up spending most of the next few evenings together. She volunteered to show me around, and I didn't want to turn down the hospitality. My parents gave Gladys a hard time for introducing us, because I didn't get to see much of them the rest of the week. No worries, since they were having a blast hanging out at the Bahia Mar Hotel, meeting my teammates and relaxing by the pool.

The week went by too quickly. I felt like I was just getting settled into my hotel room when Saturday night rolled around and we prepared to play the game of our lives the following afternoon. Practices, media events, meals, and meetings kept us on the run, and when we had a little free time, there was always someone wanting to show us around, take us on a boat ride, or just hang out. Strolling around the Bahia Mar marina with the speedboats, yachts, and party boats was a party scene—all day, every day.

The Landry Command

Our preparation on Super Bowl day was similar to that of every other game, with one exception. A six o'clock kickoff was later than our normal 1:00 p.m. and 4:00 p.m. games, so we had a few extra hours to get ready mentally and emotionally.

The locker room buzzed with guys working their way through pregame routines. Some would sit with their backs to the locker room, not making a sound; others would have quiet conversations with their teammates about game strategy; some would be manic, striding around the locker room with a wild look in their eyes like animals waiting to be unleashed; a few would head to the bathroom and throw up in the toilet, the result of adrenaline overload. I always liked visualizing what I would do when I sprinted downfield on kickoffs—where I would position myself for the best chance to make a tackle, how I would handle a double-team, what the tendencies of the Steelers' return men were based on the film we had watched over and over.

Walking onto that field on game day was like a dream come true. The stadium lights were on even though it wasn't dark yet, and the flashes from thousands of camera made it look like midday.

I'm really here. This is what all the work, the pain, the preparation, the sacrifice was about.

Exactly one year before, I had been in Boone, North Carolina, with Spalding, disinterestedly watching the game and having a good time with friends, never imagining that I'd be on the field to take on Pittsburgh in the biggest game of my life, suited up and ready to hit someone on the opening kickoff in front of the entire sporting world.

Coach Ditka approached me in the moments before kickoff.

"Are you ready to play, son?"

"Yes, sir," I shouted without hesitation, like a young recruit standing face-to-face with a drill sergeant. In those tense moments, it felt good to have Ditka there, the authority figure who could point me in the right direction, wind me up, and let me go. I felt good in my skin and knew that if my teammates and I took care of business, stayed disciplined and played within ourselves, then we had a very good chance of repeating as Super Bowl champs.

Ditka then said something that only Mike Ditka could say. He was direct. He never pulled any punches. He was always on edge as if he was preparing to play the game himself. With fire in his eyes and the passion most people know Mike Ditka for, he said, "Coach Landry told me to tell you that you better not get a penalty in this game. Those fifteen yards could be the difference. I want you putting people on their backs, but be sure you do it between whistles. And one more thing. Get a penalty, and your ass is walking back to Dallas. Got it?"

He slapped me on the helmet hard enough to make me angry and growled something at me—he always growled at players, and no one ever had the guts to ask him to repeat himself. I knew he wasn't joking. If I cost the team field position and a score because of another stupid penalty, I'd volunteer to walk back to Dallas, just to keep Ditka from tearing my leg off and beating me with it.

I stared at him for a short minute to see if he had more words. He didn't.

"No way, Coach. I mean, sure Coach. I mean, I'll guarantee you no penalties.

What else am I supposed to say?

"Oh, and I won't be walking home."

Drew Pearson

None of the receivers got hurt during the regular season, so my game time was limited—one of the downsides to playing on a championship-caliber team. During the second half of the Super Bowl, though, Drew Pearson was shaken up on a hard hit and came out of the game for a few plays.

It was third down and an obvious passing down. On that particular pass play, my route was an in-route where I would run across the middle fifteen yards from the line of scrimmage. I was running my route, and Roger, who had thrown the ball to me hundreds of times during practice, watched me come open across the middle.

He looked off. Tony Hill was headed for the end zone.

He looked back at me.

Then at Tony.

Then back at me.

And finally, after what seemed like an eternity, Roger heaved the ball in Tony Hill's direction. Tony was tied up in triple coverage, so we were fortunate the ball just fell incomplete.

It wasn't my place to mention it to Roger at the time, but several months later playing basketball at the gym, when the excitement of the day had worn off a little, I said, "Roger, you know I would've made the catch if you'd just have thrown it. How come you looked at me, looked at Tony, and then looked back at me before throwing it into a crowd?"

He stared me down and, with his deadpan sense of humor, said, "Robert, I wasn't expecting to see you there. You weren't supposed to be there. Drew was."

Roger was expecting to see Drew Pearson coming open across the middle. We had a laugh about that moment and the fact that I didn't have a single pass thrown my way during the regular season—despite supposedly having the best hands on the team. In that moment, Roger decided instead to throw into a crowd. The situation was a great disappointment for me in that I was wide open and could have—would have—made the catch. But I knew Roger did what he thought was the right thing to do. And I believed it as well.

#82, Not #81

At halftime, Pittsburgh led 21–14. The Steelers opened the scoring on Terry Bradshaw's twenty-eight-yard pass play to John Stallworth, but we came back with a Staubach to Tony Hill score and a fumble recovery for a touchdown by Mike Hegman. Stallworth caught another touchdown pass—this one seventy-five yards, the longest completion for a touchdown in Super Bowl history to that point—and Pittsburgh added a late go-ahead on a short pass to running back Rocky Bleier. The game was certainly as advertised.

In the locker room during the break, the offense huddled on one side and the defense on the other. We knew what the respective units had to do. Pittsburgh was tough—they had finished the regular season 14–2 and had manhandled the Broncos and the Oilers in the play-offs to get to the Super Bowl—but we were two evenly matched teams. Despite the fact that Hall of Fame coach Chuck Noll (who would go on to win four Super Bowls before retiring to make way for Bill Cowher) was on the other sideline guiding the Steelers, we still thought we had the coaching advantage.

We believed in Coach Landry, and we knew he believed in us.

Coach pulled the team together and talked about the season's final thirty minutes, asking us to remember the goal we had set all the way back in training camp—to play to the best of our ability and, because of our preparation and our commitment to team, to make it back to the Super Bowl.

We had accomplished one goal. Now it was time to focus for one more half of football and win the game. Complete our mission.

Coach Landry commended the Steelers on being a well-coached team. We were, he told us, in the fight of our lives. He talked of the breaks in every game and how we had to take advantage of every situation. He talked about the complete game—offense, defense, and special teams. He spoke of the need to make big plays.

But most of all, he talked about leaving everything on the field.

Coach Landry's words focused us and gave us the edge we needed.

Toward the end of an otherwise scoreless third quarter, we had driven the ball down the field on the Steelers' vaunted "Steel Curtain" defense, making it look surprisingly easy. Tony Dorsett was instrumental in getting us into the red zone, and on a third-down play from inside the Steelers' ten-yard-line, Staubach saw Jackie Smith break wide open in the end zone. In one of the most famous plays in Super Bowl history (or any other NFL game, for that matter), Smith dropped the pass that would have tied the game.

We settled for a field goal that pulled us to within four, 28–24, but the wind had been taken out of our sails. While a single play doesn't win or lose ballgames, there's no question that momentum can change—quickly and decisively—when big things happen, either good or bad.

For those few minutes, the momentum had shifted our way.

We had marched onto the doorstep, and we were knocking on the door. Getting points on a drive is rarely a bad thing, but nothing keeps momentum rolling like a touchdown.

I felt sorry for Jackie, and I knew he was sick about what happened. He was—and still is—one of the great tight ends of all time, in impeccable shape and focused on the task at hand. And it just happened. Sometimes, there's no explanation for something like that except . . . *it was what it was.*

Jackie would've caught that ball ninety-nine times out of one hundred, and every player on the Cowboys would've bet a good portion of their paycheck that he wouldn't have dropped that pass. We had practiced it many times, and Jackie never dropped the pass in practice. By allowing the ball to get to his pads, though, he violated the cardinal rule of receiving: *Keep the ball away from your body. Catch the ball with your hands and arms extended.*

Receivers sometimes try to swallow the ball with their bodies as an extra measure of protection. The problem is, when the ball hits your body and your pads, you can't predict how it will react. Since Jackie had played for the Saint Louis Cardinals for nineteen seasons without ever making it to the Super Bowl, this was his chance to show the world how great a tight end he really was. Jackie has probably replayed that play over in his mind thousands of times in the last thirty years.

In the end, he made a mistake. But that mistake didn't cost us the game. It just allowed the Steelers to recapture the momentum we had been building for much of the third quarter.

For many months after that game, people would come up to me and say, "I know you must feel horrible about dropping that pass."

"I didn't drop that pass," I'd tell them patiently, knowing what's coming next.

"But you're number eighty-one."

"No, I *was* eighty-one. Now I'm eighty-two."

That conversation repeated itself like *Groundhog Day*, since all my media pictures showed me wearing #81. I fielded way too many phone calls and conversations from friends about the "drop."

In the end, in a game widely remembered as the best Super Bowl in history—and certainly one with more Hall of Fame players than any other—we lost 35–31.

After the game, the locker room was like a morgue. Reporters hovered around the key players—Benny Barnes, Roger Staubach, Jackie Smith, Randy White, the usual suspects.

Jackie was beside himself. Generally in a locker room after a big loss, the players want to be left alone as each rewinds and plays the game tape over and over in his mind.

Could I have done anything different to affect the outcome of the game?

Were we as prepared as we needed to be?

The questions from the media were the standard questions. But this was no ordinary game. For every Cowboy, that was their last Super Bowl as a team in the Landry era. For some, it was their last game in a Cowboys uniform.

For a few others, including Jackie Smith, the game was their last as a player.

The after-game get-together, in a huge tent on the grounds of the Bahia Mar property, reminded me more of a wake than a party. Jackie Smith was nowhere to be found. Fewer than twenty of the forty-five players made an appearance. The coaches were all there because they were told they had to be there. But no one wanted to be there.

Our season was over.

It was time to reflect on the season—despite losing the Super Bowl, it would be hard to say that it had been a total disaster—take a few weeks off and begin preparing for next season.

Life would go on.

The flight back to Dallas the next morning was quieter than the typical flight home after a loss. Coach Landry made a few more remarks, similar to his comments immediately after the Super Bowl, about how well the Steelers had played and how there was no shame in losing to a team of that quality. Coach complimented the entire Steelers organization for their win. He vowed to work harder and prepare more thoroughly for next season.

With that, the Braniff plane rose up into the morning sky and headed west toward Dallas and an uncertain future.

The Super Bowl—and my season in Dallas—was a memory.

Red Zone Rules

A Man Ahead of His Time

"Coach Landry made us. We were disciplined, worked hard. We were innovative. I could take Coach Landry's playbook from the 1970s right now and run it as an offensive coordinator in the NFL today and be successful," says Drew Pearson.

"That's how innovative he was. He was the man. He set the tempo. If we wanted to be a part of the Dallas Cowboys, it was up to us to please him. The way to please him was, first, to know what you had to do, know your assignments, know your role on the team and what was expected of you.

"Second, you went out there and you did it. It was that simple. If you did it, you were fine. If you didn't, you got an opportunity to correct it. If you didn't correct it, you were gone."

Give and Take

Whatever you do, wherever you go, you should always maintain a high level of respect for others and for yourself. Treat others the way you want to be treated. Give respect, and you'll receive respect in kind.

When you reach that huge dream you've been working toward, just as I reached my dream of playing in the Super Bowl for the Dallas Cowboys, savor the moment. It's a biggie. For me, that was the game of my life. Winning or losing mattered, but it didn't matter nearly as much as just being there. I will hold the memories of that game with me forever.

And when you do experience a loss, like we lost to the Steelers, remember one thing—it's not the end of the world. Maybe it's the end of an era, or a season, or a way of life, but it's definitely not the end of the world.

New opportunities will come your way. Always be ready to seize them.

A word of advice on investments or any business decision: weigh your options carefully.

My brother had stayed with me in the Bahia Mar Hotel during the run-up to the Super Bowl, and I can say now that I think the only reason he stayed in the room with me was to ask me for my Super Bowl check. He had founded a limousine company in Columbus that was experiencing some financial troubles, and as the week wore on, he started to pitch me on becoming his partner.

"I need to be part-owner of a limousine company like I need a hole in the head," I told him. My reply was lighthearted, but my intention was deadly serious.

Still, he was my brother.

The payments I received from the divisional play-offs and the Super Bowl were about what I had made during the regular season. When my brother asked me to invest $10,000 in the business, I never gave it a second thought.

I should have.

The investment turned out to be one of my worst, but it helped my brother keep his business which he eventually moved to Atlanta. I did get a few free limo rides being an investor, but paying retail would have been a whole lot cheaper in the long run.

Deep down inside, I knew better than to invest in my brother's limousine business. I should have stuck with that gut feeling.

Are You . . . *Too?*

"It's a hard road, a tough road. But don't let anyone tell you that you can't do it," says Drew Pearson. "Don't let anybody tell you that you're too slow, you're too short, you're *too* anything.

"If you want to do it, give your best effort every time out. If I'd listened to people, or if Robert Steele had listened to everyone who tried to tell him that playing for the Cowboys was a pipe dream, that he may as well just stay at home and enjoy his life after college, neither one of us would've made it in the NFL.

"When I think what might have happened if I had never tried, that scares me a whole lot more than the thought of giving it my best shot and failing. Inaction is the worst kind of failure."

A Winner's Mindset

"Every member of the Dallas Cowboys had the expectation that they would be in the play-offs and could get to the Super Bowl," says Bruce Huther. "When I played for other teams, too often my teammates would look forward to the last game of the season, just play out the string, so they could go home.

"The mindset of a winner—that's a totally different feeling."

14

Off-Season Fun

Kenneth Cooper Clinic

One day, the Cowboys' trainer told me I needed to get my body fat tested.

Body fat? Me?

Kenneth H. Cooper, MD, MPh, published *Aerobics* in 1968, introducing a new exercise concept to America. Dr. Cooper became well known in preventative medicine and sports medicine over the next four decades.

In 1979, the Cowboys went to Dr. Cooper's clinic to test players' overall body condition, including body fat percentages. The assessments included the caliper that grabs your skin and measures fat, as well as twenty other tests, including a water-displacement test. Doctors and trainers believed that all of those evaluations taken together revealed important facts about body mass and lean-to-fat ratios and would eventually lead to better and more efficient ways to train for what was becoming a more competitive and, in many ways, a more violent game.

After holding my breath for one minute, naked, in a tank of water, I was surprised when they told me that my percentage of body fat was the lowest in testing history for the Cowboys. I knew I was lean at six foot four and 199 pounds. I got a little concerned, though, when the doctor said, "Are you aware that, according to our charts, you're too thin?"

"Ah, I don't think so. What are you talking about?" Couldn't say I cared for his line of questioning.

"Well, we've never had anybody come in here with their body fat under 2 percent. Preston Pearson was the lowest at 2.1 percent, and you're clicking in at"—the doctor looked down at his clipboard to confirm and, with a look of surprise on his face, repeated the number—"1.9 percent." (Of course, those percentages come when you work out ten hours a day, every day. There's no fat left. From what I understand, that record still holds.)

"Look, I drink milkshakes every day. I eat pretty much everything I want to eat. I don't know how many calories I take in, but I'm sure it's four or five thousand a day."

"Well, you're burning probably about eight thousand. You have such lean body mass that you don't have a lot of protection around the muscles. Makes it a whole lot easier to get hurt when you don't have anything to protect you from a direct hit."

I knew I needed my speed and quickness—my edge on the playing field—and having a few extra pounds would only slow me down. "So shouldn't I be proud of this?" I asked.

The doctor just shook his head. "You're obviously very fit," he said. "But a few extra pounds could only help."

"OK, I will work on that," was all I could muster.

Hollywood Henderson

Because of my work ethic, I was always at the Cowboys training facility. Some of my teammates joked that I should put a cot in the locker room so that I could just roll out of bed and already be in the weight room. I pushed myself, feeling that I needed to do more every single day because the coaches kept statistics on everything—even how many workouts a player did in the off-season.

My efforts didn't shock the coaches, who had seen my workout schedule over the last year. I was surprised to find out, though, that some of the players didn't like my work ethic. Hollywood Henderson was one of them.

One of the most interesting encounters I had while playing for the Cowboys was on a summer day a few months before we returned to the 1979 training camp. Out of nowhere, Hollywood walked into the locker room and looked at the chart keeping stats on workout attendance. He made an off-the-cuff remark about my perfect attendance. I explained to him that I needed the extra workouts. The comment just seemed to make him angry.

"Rookie," he spit, getting up in my face and trying to back me down, "you better know who I am and what I mean to this team. I ain't going to work out any more than I have to, because I am perfect. You may have perfect attendance, but I am *perfect*! You got that?"

Hollywood was an All-Pro linebacker, but the glazed look in his eyes told me he had had more than orange juice or coffee to wake up that day. I didn't back down, and a brawl ensued.

"I'll whip your ass," he yelled.

"Rookie, maybe. But I'm not afraid of you," I shouted back at him.

In the midst of all that shoving, pushing, fighting, and slugging, other players intervened, separating us like boys tussling in a schoolyard. With a couple of guys holding each of us back, I looked Hollywood straight in the eye.

"I don't think you understand. I don't give a shit who you are, Henderson."

We both backed off with some encouragement from the other players, and I think Hollywood started to pay attention to this punk rookie wide receiver who spent too much time in the weight room. We exchanged a few more choice words, and he swore at me the whole way out of the locker room.

Oddly, Hollywood and I became much closer as a result of that encounter. The next day we met, shook hands, and Hollywood acted like a totally different person.

Could it have been the drugs in his system the day before?

Probably, because the next day he was all smiles, wanting to show everyone that we were friends and that he respected the rookie.

I certainly respected Hollywood's playing abilities. As a former number one draft choice (always on the lookout for new talent, Gil Brandt had spotted Henderson at Langston University, an Oklahoma school with fewer than four thousand students), he had the ability to back up his mouth, and he was one of the most feared defensive ends in the league for a decade.

I just wanted him to see me not as a scared little boy, but as one of his peers.

He respected that, and we never had another cross word.

Glen Carano, Workout Partner

One of my favorite teammates was Glen Carano, a third-string Cowboys quarterback drafted in 1977. Glen and I were workout partners, and he knew that I would run as many pass patterns as he needed to get his timing down for the other receivers. Almost daily, we worked out by running every pass pattern in the Cowboys playbook. Our routine allowed me to earn Glen's confidence and, by extension, the confidence of the other quarterbacks, Roger

Staubach and Danny White. They all knew that I would be there to help them get better, even though I might never catch a pass from them in a game.

I ran almost a thousand pass patterns during my eighteen months with the Cowboys. Glen rewarded my dedication by having me over to dinner with him and his wife. She cooked up delicious Italian dishes, and I never turned down an invitation from them.

Perks

Hanging out in Dallas in the off season, as a member of the Cowboys, came with more than a few rewards. We all had unlimited opportunities for theater tickets, golf tournaments, dinners, charity basketball games, pool parties, live radio remotes—and even occasional invitations from female staff to become more acquainted with the Dallas scenery.

Quite a few of the Cowboys played in charity basketball games within a fifty- or sixty-mile radius of Dallas, sometimes getting paid several hundred dollars to show up for a game. Most players enjoyed the charity circuit (the off-season conditioning that basketball gave us didn't hurt either) and donated those funds back to the charity.

Besides, those games had benefits of their own. Cowboys groupies were some of the prettiest women anywhere.

Who could argue?

Being entertained and playing pro football for a living seemed like too much fun and not what I would have expected from my first job.

One of the more enjoyable events was the Gatlin Brothers Golf Tournament at the Loew's Anatole Hotel. The Gatlin brothers knew how to throw a party, and they always invited celebrities from the football and entertainment industries.

Getting to fly in a helicopter to the golf course was a real treat. Attending the star-studded gala, a glitzy event I'd never before experienced in my young life, was pretty special for me.

The distractions that I never knew existed the previous summer seemed to come along every day. Now, I knew why the players did not show up to the workout facility as much as I had the year before. There was always something to do, some event to attend, a party wanting your attendance. Every day could be filled with more parties than you could ever attend. But I kept working out.

Ditka's Long Drive

At one of those many charity golf tournaments, about forty players, among them Coach Ditka, played at one of the Club Corp courses in Dallas. Like most, the tournament had a prize for the longest drive on the eighteenth, a long straight hole. I wasn't much of a golfer at the time, but I did enjoy hitting the ball a long way, using my height and a large swing arc to generate good club-head speed. My only problem was that I tended to land the ball in the wrong zip code for the hole I was playing.

That day was an exception.

The long-drive hole was a straight 375-yard par four with a slight downhill run to the green. I didn't know it was the contest hole when I teed off, so I didn't try to kill the drive. I crushed it with a draw—a slight right-to-left turn—that only increased the drive's distance. When I got to the ball, I saw it had come to rest some fifty yards in front of the previous long drive. I walked back to the marker to record my name and noticed that the last name on the sign was Ditka's.

I wrote my name down and moved along.

Ditka was always competitive and often won the long-drive competition in the local tournaments he played. When the tournament was over, we all sat with our teammates at long tables, eating chicken and beef from the buffet and waiting for the scores and prizes to be announced. When the announcer got to awarding the prize for long drive, Coach Ditka got up from his seat and headed toward the podium.

"And the long-drive winner is . . . Robert Steele."

Ditka turned around and watched me as I walked to the podium to pick up my reward, a dozen golf balls. It wasn't the golf balls, of course, that made the prize sweet, but the fact that Ditka looked like somebody had just told him his dog had been run over.

"There's no way you out-drove me on that hole, Steele." I shouldn't have been surprised that it came out more as a growl than a statement. I wondered if he even sounded like that at home, talking to his wife and kids.

"Coach, I knocked it by you. Probably on the fly." I shrugged my shoulders and added, "Just luck, I guess."

When the guys sitting around us heard me tell Ditka that I'd airmailed his tee shot, they started oohing and aahing. The game was on. And when Ditka thought I was showing him up, he was pissed.

"I'm telling you, Steele, that's bullshit. There's no way you hit it by me on that hole." His face turned red, and he gripped the back of a chair hard enough that his knuckles turned white—but his knuckles weren't as pale as the face of the guy sitting in the chair.

Ditka looked around, didn't get any support from his fellow players, and cursed a couple more times. Turning back toward me, he looked down at my shoes, football cleats with specialized soles to improve my traction on the Astroturf field. I didn't own a pair of golf shoes at the time.

Ditka let rip. "Let me tell you something, Steele. I better not catch you playing golf again in those shoes. If I ever see you out on another golf course in those shoes, I'll send you home. Count on it."

It was all he had, and by that time, I was feeling kind of sorry for him.

"Yes, sir," I said, nodding as he turned away from my table. I sat down amid a smattering of applause from the guys I had played with.

Someone in the back of the room hollered, "Hey, Ditka, why don't you sit down and stop crying. The kid hit it past you. *Way* past you." Ditka's head snapped around.

More hoots and hollers.

"Come up here and tell me that, you son of a bitch," he shouted toward the table. He couldn't pin it on anybody in particular, which incensed him even more.

Silence.

I watched Ditka's garishly colored golf sweater disappear through the door as he stalked away. I knew, once he got over the small slight I had given him by joining in a little fun at his expense, he had taken the high road. At that moment, he would have liked nothing more than to come across the table and turn me inside out. I admired the fact that the competitive fire didn't burn any less hot, even with his playing days long behind him.

The next day I was at the workout facility when Ditka walked out of the racquetball court. He then asked if I wanted to play. He spent the next thirty minutes giving me a racquetball lesson I never forgot. He never moved from the middle of the court, and I chased the ball from side to side. I could tell he enjoyed kicking my butt. Ditka's competitive fire burned as hot as anybody I had ever met.

I certainly wasn't surprised when just a handful of years later, Ditka led the Chicago Bears to one of the great seasons in NFL history, cementing his reputation as not only a Hall of Fame player, but a coach that his mentor Tom Landry could be proud of.

Cheerleaders

Every red-blooded boy in America knew the Dallas Cowboys cheerleaders, the delightful distractions of every game. Gil Brandt told me when I arrived in Dallas after making the team that the cheerleaders had a written rule that the players were "off limits." Any cheerleader seen with a player would be terminated immediately. The players didn't have such an edict, but I can verify that the cheerleaders were nowhere to be found.

This wasn't the case, though, with the infamous—and immensely popular—former Cowboys cheerleaders who posed for *Playboy*. They showed up at many of our events and were usually available for dinner or drinks after any of the events. They were always willing to be your hostess when friends and family came to town.

I tended to spend what little free time I had not looking for Cowboys cheerleaders, but seeking the company of the LA Rams cheerleaders and Miami Dolphin cheerleaders, who didn't seem to have any problems fraternizing with players from another team when they were in town.

Those ladies were fair game.

The Breaks

In the off-season, players were more relaxed about their training schedule. No one was fighting for his job, and every player—with a few exceptions—was professional enough to stay in some semblance of conditioning so that the upcoming training camp wouldn't be like a weeks-long forced march.

One morning, running back Robert Newhouse was in the weight room with us. Newhouse, whose career with the Cowboys spanned twelve years, was built like a fireplug. At 5'10" and 220 pounds, his low center of gravity made it nearly impossible to tackle him above the waist, and any linebacker trying to get low

Red Zone Rules

Work the Network

"Robert had really outstanding character. He was a very, very competitive individual," says Gil Brandt. "Some people say they are competitive, and they are competitive to a certain level. Robert was one of those guys who no matter what walk of life he would have entered, he was going to be successful.

"The thing I remember most about Robert Steele was his ability to interact with players. He was a very, very popular player because the guy was just a person who had real good people skills. In any event of life, people skills and the ability to develop relationships will serve you well."

Living the Life

When you're doing your life's work, you'll meet a number of people from all walks of life. Take the time to get to know these people. Sometimes you may hit it off great from the start. Other times you might have a rocky beginning, the way Hollywood Henderson and I did. But with everyone you encounter, you have the opportunity to build a relationship. Treat everyone you meet as a potential friend.

Welcome the new experiences that come your way. As a Dallas Cowboy, I got to play golf, attend glitzy parties, and attend charity benefits—all kinds of wonderful experiences. I welcomed those experiences and tried to make the most of them.

Belong

"The Cowboys' philosophy was that we answered phone calls. We answered mail. We tried to make people accountable," says Gil Brandt.

"In training camp, I had eight scouts, and we would assign each one of those scouts to certain players. So when they went to lunch, for example, one of my guys would talk to Robert. Not about football, necessarily, but more along the lines of 'Robert, can we help you in any way? You have any problems? How is everything at home?'

"We knew a little bit about all our players' histories—if they were married or single, if they had a sister or a brother. We used to do those kinds of things to interact with the players. We thought it would be good for morale. It can get very lonely in training camp when you're there and somebody yells, 'Hey you,' or 'Eighty-two, where you goin' on that route?'"

The Cowboys paid attention to details that most other organizations did not see as important. Everything was important. Everything mattered. We were America's Team, and it showed.

Feel the Burn

Competition.

It's the fire in your soul.

It's that driving desire to win.

You don't need to put others down on your way to the top. On the contrary, bring them along. You get to the top in large part through that competitive spirit, that deep-seated desire and drive to win.

15

1979 Training Camp

A New Season

I was anxious for 1979 to begin. This was going to be my breakout year. I was no longer a rookie. I would be issued white pants and a locker in the varsity locker room with my teammates and given the opportunity to watch the rookies of 1979 tested as we had been the previous year.

Once the Super Bowl hangover had worn off—hangover in the sense that, after working toward a goal and coming up just short, every player on the team had to recharge mentally more than physically—we had little time to prepare for our preseason games. We were scheduled to play in the Hall of Fame game in Canton, Ohio, in about four weeks.

I was nervous about the upcoming season. I was in great shape, having prepared as hard—or maybe even a bit harder—than I had the year before, but I sensed that my "sophomore" season with the Cowboys would present challenges that I couldn't have anticipated as a rookie, when everything just flew by and I hung on for the ride. I only had six weeks to prepare for 1978 and almost six months for the 1979 season. I wanted to make every moment count.

I would return to Thousand Oaks and the Cal Lutheran campus as determined as last year to make the team, win my game ball, and become more of a contributor to the team. Maybe even make my first reception.

Hollywood Henderson arrived at camp in true "Hollywood" fashion. I came to camp a few days early to workout with the quarterbacks before the full squad arrived. The QBs and I were on the field when a stretch limo pulled into the lot next to the facility. Hollywood climbed out with an entourage big enough to make even today's celebrities jealous.

He was sending a not-too-subtle message to Coach Landry. *I'm one of your stars. You can't be successful without me. It's Hollywood Henderson's universe, and you're just renting space.*

I looked over at Coach Landry and was touched by the disappointed expression he had on his face, as though the mob scene accompanying the player's arrival had somehow cheapened everything Hollywood had worked for as a player and a man. (Coach Landry's reaction seemed prescient four years later when, in 1983, Hollywood was arrested for possession of crack cocaine before becoming an outspoken drug-treatment advocate.)

Coach quickly turned back to the business at hand—helping the rookies and a few veterans to get better every day—as if nothing had happened.

The media were a little less tenacious in 1979. While the Dallas Cowboys were still being marketed as "America's Team," we were no longer the World Champions. We were number two. Like Avis, we had to try harder. Training camp—and even Cal Lutheran's crappy food—felt good once again.

Men's Buns

During training camp, an odd rumor circulated around the practice facility. A female journalist was writing a book, and she wanted to take photographs and talk with a few of the players. Since I wasn't one of the stars, I never gave it a second thought.

A year and a half later, though, an ex-girlfriend called my house in Columbus, Georgia. "Congratulations! You're famous!" she told me, laughing. "Or at least your buns are."

"Great. Ah, what are we talking about here?"

She told me about a book called *A Woman's Look at Men's Buns,* by Christie Jenkins. To my knowledge, I had never posed for any photographs and didn't deserve this newfound fame.

I asked my sister to go out and find a copy of the book. She went over to White's Bookstore and, of course, it wasn't on the shelf of the conservative hometown store. So, she ordered it. When I saw the book, it took me a little by surprise. The men's buns were in various stages of undress, but most of them were clothed or partially clothed. The author did a tasteful view of the subject. I was photographed from a distance, a rear view shot, and totally unaware the picture was even being taken. The very tight sweat pants were what she wanted to shoot. Thankfully, I wasn't exposing my full glory on the practice field.

The book credits suggested she only took pictures of friends and friends of friends, but I had never met Christie. One fact I'm most proud of is that I'm fully dressed in my Cowboy sweats, and my back is turned to the camera. I wasn't the star, but Christie chose my "buns" over those of the better-known guys on the team.

Training camp was officially opening for 1979, and Coach Landry wanted to see us return to the Super Bowl and win this year. Of course, that never happened again. I spent extra time with teammates, as I had the previous year, running the offense until it became second nature and practicing pass routes with the quarterbacks. Glen Carano and I, especially, spent a lot of time preparing for the upcoming season. My legs would last as long as his arm was good, and I was pleased that every once in a while, a small group of guys would stop what they were doing and watch us practice, as if to say, *Those two have got it right. That's what we talk about when we talk about work ethic.*

Glen didn't have an off-season job, so he was really working on moving up the depth chart—a monumental task, considering Danny White, Roger Staubach's backup, would have started for most other NFL franchises.

In fact, Glen never did make the jump, but he became an accomplished quarterback in his own right and played in the United States Football League for the Pittsburgh Maulers. Overall, he had a good career, just not what he expected when he signed with the Cowboys out of Las Vegas.

I look back on those early days of the second training camp fondly. I never got tired or even broke into a hard sweat. Of course, when I found out about the low body fat reading, I knew why I didn't sweat. I had no fat to burn off.

Mentally, I got very good at setting goals and working to meet my own expectations as the underdog. No matter what successes came to me, I knew I had to do more. I trained equally hard in the second training camp as I had in the first, going full speed in every drill, every practice, every single time I stepped on the field.

Some of the guys started acting like they were popping pills—trying to get me to let them in on my private stash. After several repeated pill popping gestures, I finally asked them what they were doing.

"What're *we* doing? What're *you* doing, Steele? Ain't nobody goes the way you go all the time that ain't on something. We'd like to know what *you're* on."

So I was getting called out by the same guys I knew had been taking pills.

What can you do? I went out and did my job.

I can only look back and laugh, since the media had a heyday with some Cowboys who used drugs later. I'm proud that I've never put any performance-enhancing drug in my body.

I think about the guys who were insecure enough to get involved with steroids to make themselves bigger or faster. On the other hand, I was afraid if I did anything, I would mess up and it would cost me my position. I didn't want to drink a beer. Nothing went in to my body that might derail my workout efforts. The whole story points out what was wrong with the culture of professional football, because the perception was that anybody able to keep up a strenuous regimen on the practice field and in the weight room couldn't have done it without an aid or a crutch—which I can say from experience is false and a real disservice to the players who stayed clean for their whole careers.

I share in my inspirational talks the idea that there's a fine line between a starter and the superstars, whether in athletics or business. What separates those groups is the mental aspect of the game and how willing you are to be true to yourself, to raise the bar for yourself, and to leverage the tools you were given without resorting to cheating. It is possible to be clean, strong, and straight.

For example, in training camp, coaches test your mental mettle every day through game reviews, repetition of plays, and your physical and mental conditioning and agility.

Keeping on top of my game required fitness beyond most people's capabilities. I never got physically tired. I never got mentally tired. And that required focus on every play, every day.

Rafael Septien's Kicking Instructions

Coach Landry invited his good friend Ben Agajanian, who was the first kicking specialist in pro football, to Thousand Oaks to work with the Cowboys during each training camp. Ben had developed a relationship with kicker Rafael Septien, who came to Dallas from Los Angeles and would spend eight years with the Cowboys. Ben spent time coaching Rafael's skills, and since I was the holder I got to hear all of the teaching moments as well. It's funny looking at the kickers today with the device that holds the ball for them while they practice their kicks. We did not have those back then, and every kick had to be held physically by another player. Rafael did not like practicing with the tee used for kickoffs, so he and I practiced kicking for hours on end.

One afternoon while Rafael and I were practicing together, Ben decided to give me a little coaching lesson. Coach Landry had walked over to our area when Ben said, "Robert, I just want you to know one thing. If Rafael doesn't get it to the goal post, that's his fault, but if he misses it to the right or the left, then that's on you."

Coach went on to explain that if I tilted the ball—that is, if it weren't perfectly vertical when Rafael's foot hit it—then the ball could go to the left or right, much like a hooked or sliced golf shot.

Of course, they expected me to make it perfect every single time. Ben's comment in front of Coach Landry was no accident. I should, Ben implied, never make a mistake. Hold it perfectly, in under a second, with eleven crazy guys (they were special teams players, after all, looking to make a name for themselves) surging through the line like rabid wolves looking for fresh meat trying to block the kick.

Simple enough. No pressure there.

Since Rafael and I were taught the same rules by the same coach, I was surprised by his response to a question many years later. Rafael was asked why he missed a kick. His not-so-perfect-English response: "The holder put the ball upside down." Of course, a football has no wrong end. Upside down to Rafael was his life, not the football.

Classic. Only a kicker could ever come up with that excuse.

Don't Work Out So Hard, Underdog

I spent so much time working out that I knew an injury, though possible, was less likely for me than most of my teammates. I was in great shape.

Still, I wasn't prepared for a hit to my lower back as I stretched for an errant pass from one of our rookie quarterbacks. I went all-out for every pass, because I now had a reputation for catching almost every pass. In this case, that reputation worked against me. I went up to snatch the ball, which was three or four feet higher than it should have been, and took a hammer shot straight to my lower back by a rookie defensive back doing his job. I was bent almost in half, backward. The pain was both immediate and intense.

I lay on the ground for almost ten minutes thinking I might have broken my back. When I was able to pick myself up, the trainers insisted that I go to the local hospital for X-rays. I got back to the Cal Lutheran campus in time for roll call at the evening meetings. Coach told me to go to the dorm to rest, but I couldn't afford to miss anything new that might be introduced that evening. I was in extreme pain as I sat through the evening meetings. And because I didn't think I had any room to lag around, I was at practice bright and early the next morning.

The pain was unbearable. I looked around and counted fifteen players in camp gunning for my spot. Some were free agents with the hope (small as it was) of making the team, like I had been, as well as two draft choices. I knew I couldn't afford to miss a practice, much less a preseason game.

I played the entire preseason in excruciating pain. When we were in the locker room prior to the July preseason Hall of Fame game against the Oakland Raiders in Canton, Ohio, the team doctor, Pat Evans, offered novocain to help get me up on my feet.

I'll take shots in the back, if it'll get me through the game.

Dr. Evans tapped out a dose of Novocain and stuck the long needle into my spine. A few players told me I was crazy, that I could hurt my back permanently, like the Patriots' Darryl Stingley had (even though Stingley's paraplegia came as the result of a forearm shiver by Oakland headhunting defensive back Jack Tatum in a preseason game the year before).

The Hall of Fame game was the only one in which I was not able to turn fast enough to catch a pass thrown slightly behind me. Having a pass thrown my way was my way to shine, and I never wanted to ever drop a single ball. Turning as best as I could, I managed to get a hand on the errant throw and knock it down. I felt like I would have adjusted better had my back not hurt so bad. I managed to play through the pain and spent the next six months crawling out of bed each morning, resigned to the notion that I was another in the growing line of NFL players who would deal with injury on a daily basis just to play a little boys' game. I knew I would do anything to keep my spot on the roster, and I spent the better part of the summer in the whirlpool and with ice packs, trying to stay on the practice field.

A little humor to my pain that preseason was the ribbing I got from Tony Hill, Drew Pearson, and Butch Johnson about my perfect-attendance workout schedule: "It's a good thing we didn't keep Robert's workout schedule," they would say, "or we'd be the ones hurt." They kept giving Ditka a hard time about my 100 percent attendance to the practice facility and 100 percent attendance in the training room.

A Raise

It's a rare event indeed when your team or your company tells you that you aren't earning enough money, so I was surprised when Gil Brandt asked me to come to his office prior to the final preseason game.

"Coach Landry wants to increase your salary to $30,000 this season and $35,000 for next season," Gil said. "We hope you don't mind."

"Thanks," I said, shocked that it should be that easy to get a raise anywhere, let alone from an NFL franchise. "Don't mind at all."

I would never make superstar money—I had accepted that when I saw a guy like Hollywood Henderson roll up in a limo with his entourage and all the trappings of the high-dollar lifestyle—but Gil Brandt's message made me feel good about being a member of the Dallas Cowboys: *We appreciate the effort you make, and we value your contribution to the team.*

Maybe the Cowboys would keep me around for a couple more years, since I was supposed to make $25,000 my second year. I was the still going to be the lowest paid player on the team, but that was OK by me.

I was glad to be in Dallas. Steele here.

The Beginning of the End

Toward the wrap-up of camp, three of our six running backs were injured. Final cuts were coming, and the numbers were beginning to work against me. Coaches didn't want to put a starting running back on waivers, fearing that he wouldn't clear. Instead, they waited, letting the starters make the team and then placing them on injured reserve, which meant they wouldn't have to clear waivers when they were healthy again.

Those were the rules in the good old days, and teams used the loopholes to their advantage when they could. A lot of players fell through the cracks because of those rules. On the final cut, just like last year, I was not told what was going on.

The Cowboys chose to put me on waivers, which left the team with three wide receivers. Every team in the NFL knew that the Cowboys wouldn't go with three wide receivers, so there was a good chance I wouldn't clear waivers—that is, I would end up playing someplace else.

It was, I realized even then, the beginning of the end.

I had made it through the end of preseason, but eventually I got a call from the coaching staff. I wonder today if I had known who it was even before I picked up the phone.

"Robert, you need to come and see Coach Landry," the voice on the other end of the line told me. And then with just the briefest of hesitations: "And bring your playbook."

I shuddered.

Has the Turk finally come around for a visit? Was this what it felt like?

I showed up to the Cowboys headquarters. It was a short, five-minute drive from my Sandhurst Lane apartment. "We have five running backs hurt, and we need to do some roster moves, just like last year," Coach Landry said. "We placed you on waivers hoping you would not get picked up. You were picked up by the Vikings, and I want to wish you luck with your new team."

Handing Coach Landry the playbook, the one I knew from cover to cover, seemed like I was handing him my birthright or my reason to live. I paused in his office, tears about to well in my eyes, wanting to turn around and thank him for the opportunity he had given me, and I chose to keep walking. I know I would have begun to cry if I had turned around. Grown men do not cry, so I kept walking. Coach Landry had plenty to do. He did not need me to get emotional as I departed for my apartment and my next opportunity. I figured I would be able to thank him at another time. I quickly convinced myself that time would be a much better time and punched the elevator button, never to return.

I saw Todd Christenson walking out of the headquarters as well. He had been placed on waivers and was picked up by the New York Giants. Todd, the number two draft choice the previous year, was not happy, as his attitude and comments showed. "I will make the Cowboys regret this day," Christenson muttered as he got in his car. I was disappointed as well, but at least somebody wanted me. Even if it was the Minnesota Vikings. Heading back to the apartment, not sure what this next team would be like or how I would fit in, seemed to take a lot longer driving home than it did driving over.

Red Zone Rules

The Error of Your Ways

"The mental strain, the uncertainty, gets to a lot of guys. Doesn't have anything to do with physical ability," says Dan Reeves.

"*Gosh I was going to be cut?*'

"*Somebody's going to knock on the door. They're going to let some people go tonight. Will I be one of them?*'

"*I've got to spend more time with my playbook.*'

"*I can't afford to make any more mental mistakes.*'

"We would tell players that they're going to make errors. And we would also warn them not to turn *errors* into *mistakes*.

"What's the difference?

"If you repeat an error, then it becomes a mistake.

"So what you want to do is shake off the errors, but don't make the mistakes. That's mentally taxing for players and requires an incredible amount of discipline, because you've got to put the last play behind you and move forward to the next one.

"Forget about the last play, because you can't do anything about it. Just learn from it and move on."

Perspiration, Not Inspiration

"Preparation. There are an awful lot of things that go into it. First of all, it starts with getting the right kind of people, self-motivated people," says Dan Reeves. "We want people who are unselfish and playing with the team's best interest in mind. You have to surround yourself with those kinds of people, and then you've got to get them prepared.

"Coach Landry always told us that preparation is the greatest motivator, and he was never more right about anything. If we prepare our guys to the best of their ability, and they go out on the field and know they're not going to be surprised by something, then they've got a great chance to be successful."

Getting On with Your Life's Work

You've reached your big dream. Now what?

Life goes on, and you move forward. You dream new dreams, create new goals. Dreaming and doing never end.

In any endeavor—whether it's football, business, your family, or any other aspect of your life that's important to you—you've got to push yourself mentally. There will be times when your body tires, your motivation lessens, your determination fades. Those are the times when you need to rely on your mental strength more than ever.

Keeping pushing yourself!

I know people who have turned to drugs for a variety of reasons. Don't give in to the temptation. It's never worth it. Drugs can't help you, but they *will* destroy you.

Rely on preparation and your will to succeed. The more you practice, the more you learn, the more you work out your mind and your body—the better prepared you'll be when the big day comes for you to shine!

16

Purple Haze

Minnesota Vikings

Anybody else would have been thrilled, but the phone call I got next told me I had to be in Minnesota that afternoon for practice. Coach Landry told me the Minnesota Vikings had picked me up off waivers. The voice on the other end confirmed that to be true, and I needed to pack and head north.

I couldn't believe what had happened in the space of a few hours, going from a sure spot on my dream team to an outfit famous for losing Super Bowls. (Between 1969 and 1976, the Vikings made the big game four times in the span of eight years without winning, an inauspicious record bested only by the Buffalo Bills twenty years later when the team lost four consecutive Super Bowls.)

I paused as I packed, thinking about what had just happened. *The Minnesota Vikings. I don't want to play for another team. I'm happy in Dallas. Do I have a choice? Can I refuse to go? Am I just an indentured servant with no rights whatsoever?*

I asked those questions to myself and realized my choices

were clear-cut: get on a plane to Minneapolis or go home. Simple as that.

The Vikings owned the rights to my services, and I would either play for them or hang up my spikes for good. Needless to say, I wasn't happy. Most players would've been grateful for the opportunity to walk into a position on a team that, even though they hadn't won the Super Bowl, always seemed to be around come play-off time.

I, on the other hand, wanted to jump off the roof of the fourteen-story hotel where I had had my first physical for the Cowboys. I wasn't going to fit in with the Vikings. I don't know how I knew, just that my gut was telling me something was wrong.

This new phase of my NFL career was one of the most disconcerting periods of my life. When I look back on it, I realize that I wasn't really prepared mentally for such a big change so quickly. For the last year, my daily focus had been the Dallas Cowboys.

I lived, breathed, dreamed—and daydreamed—the Dallas Cowboys.

I drank the Kool-Aid, followed the rites and rituals of the Dallas Cowboys "religion." The transition to a new group mindset in Minnesota was going to be strange and difficult.

I arrived at the Vikings training camp at Minnesota State University in Mankato, Minnesota, trying to be excited about my new team. But I still wondered why the sudden change in fortune.

Why did the Vikings pick me up?

How will I be received by my new teammates?

Will I be able to turn off my love of the Cowboys and focus my efforts on helping the Vikings win games? After all, that's what they're paying me for.

I was torn emotionally by loyalty to the Cowboys and finding my place—if I had one—with the Vikings. Consciously, I knew I would have to get over leaving the Cowboys if I ever wanted to make a career in the NFL. Still, I had no idea how I was going to manage.

In my heart, I hoped the Cowboys would pick me back up, just like they had the previous year. But the Cowboys had never carried three wide receivers, and the Vikings knew that. The easiest way for the Vikings to ensure that I would never play again for the Cowboys was to pick me up off waivers—maybe the greatest backhanded compliment a player could ever get from an opponent.

My first day in camp, I met the legendary head coach Bud Grant, who led the Vikings for eighteen seasons and, at the time, was behind only Don Shula and George Halas for career NFL wins. Grant looked to be about Coach Landry's age. He saw me in the locker room and introduced himself.

"If you can't fit in here, you won't fit in anywhere," he said, giving me a firm handshake and looking me in the eye. I think he was trying to make me comfortable in my new surroundings, but I thought even at the time what an odd statement it was, especially given my later experiences with the Vikings.

Les Steckel, the second person I met, was the receivers and special teams coach, the Vikings' Ditka. Steckel would become the Vikings' head coach when Grant retired and then go to be an assistant coach on a handful of teams in the league. He was all business when he handed me the Vikings playbook.

"Learn those plays, Steele," he told me. "You won't see any action for at least two weeks, since we don't expect you to get up to speed for a while, but we already know you can help on special teams. We've seen the film."

So far, so good. Steckel seemed like a straight shooter, and I was pleased to be on special teams until I could prove myself at receiver.

Getting dressed for my first practice, I met Joe Senser, a free agent rookie tight end who had just made the team. He introduced himself and put me a little at ease. "I watched you in the Super Bowl," Senser said. "Awesome game. I'm new here, too. Let me know if I can do anything to help."

Joe was learning the system, too, and didn't have much more experience with the Vikings than I did. I appreciated his offer of help. I thought maybe things might be a little less cutthroat here than they were in Dallas—the only advantage Minnesota could ever have over my previous team.

The Vikings depth chart showed me as the second wide receiver, behind Ahmad Rashad, a talented receiver out of the University of Oregon in his fourth year with the Vikings after brief stints with Saint Louis, Buffalo, and Seattle. Rashad was a good receiver—he would finish his NFL career with almost five hundred catches—but word on the street was that he was a bit of a prima donna, something I would have a chance to witness up close and personal in the coming weeks.

The team also had Sammy White and Doug Cunningham, Tommy Kramer's college roommate from Rice University, at wide receiver. Tommy Kramer was the starting quarterback, taking over from Hall of Famer Fran Tarkenton, who had retired at the end of the previous season after compiling career stats that would stand for decades. That Kramer was Tarkenton's chosen replacement certainly didn't hurt Cunningham's chances to make the team. Everyone pulled for him to make the team and loved the fact when Coach Grant kept him over a few other players. Kramer knew Cunningham and threw to him quite a bit. But Kramer was here to make a name for himself, not help Cunningham unless it helped him. Cunningham was not fast, but he could catch the ball.

In three days, I had learned the Vikings' entire playbook and went to talk to Coach Steckel.

"Hey Coach, I'm ready to play. I've memorized the playbook." I held the dog-eared book out to him as if to prove that I knew everything between its covers.

"Robert, you've only been here three days," Steckel said, obviously skeptical at what I was telling him. He even acted a little put out that I would waste his time by coming to him so soon after my arrival, claiming to know the system that other players must have taken quite a while to learn. "I've already told Jerry Burns, our offensive coordinator, that you wouldn't know our system for about a month," Steckel continued, shrugging his shoulders.

Sure, no skin off your back if I don't get to play.

"Coach, I respect that. But I'm telling you, I already know the book. I'm ready to get out there."

To test me, Steckel called out a few plays, and I told him my assignment. He walked away, shaking his head in amazement. I had convinced him, to be sure. But I never received an answer about playing.

The opening game for the 1979 season was a few days away, and I was still trying to get excited about my new team. As hard as that was, I thought about what the Cowboys were doing every day. I missed my team. I wanted to be in Dallas, not Minneapolis.

Still, I had a job to do, and I would do it to the best of my ability. I had a goal left to accomplish—to win a game ball. Playing at the old Metropolitan stadium in Minneapolis was the pits (this was before the state-of-the-art Hubert H. Humphrey Dome was built in 1982; although I'm no fan of shopping malls, the fact that the Mall of America now sits on the site of the old Metropolitan Stadium strikes me as a nice irony). The Met was tired back then. A new shopping mall with all of the glitz and glamor would have been a much better place to play that this dump. The Major League Baseball team, the Twins, hadn't finished their season by the time we started ours, and the football field was a baseball diamond converted every Saturday for a Sunday-afternoon football game. Chunks of hastily situated sod would be kicked up—and knees and other joints torn up—because the roots hadn't had time to take hold. Hitting the infield was like landing on asphalt.

The Vikings didn't even have their own practice facility, no real home. The team met in the bottom of the stadium, the bowel as I called it, for our daily film sessions. During the late summer, when the Twins were in town, we practiced on a field at the old fairgrounds, a run-down facility that should have been razed decades before. I cut my finger on a piece of glass coming out of my stance on a snap. No wonder Ahmad never touched the ground in his stance. While the Cowboys practice facility on Forest Lane was no "showplace," it sure beat this dilapidated hellhole.

More than one of my teammates agreed. If I had a dollar for every time somebody mumbled about "this shitty field" on the way out of a practice, I could have retired by the end of the season.

Making Adjustments

I did my best to fit in with the Vikings culture, becoming friends with several of the new players on the team, including Kurt Knoff and Frank Myers, moving into a house south of town, in Burnsville. Suburbia was not a bad place to live, but it was certainly not "The Village" in Dallas, where all the singles lived and frequented the nightspots nearby. Frank, Kurt, and I became fast friends because we all had played on a previous team and were new to the Viking culture. Kurt and I shared multiple knee surgeries and funny looking legs. I laughed when I saw his knees the first time and told him he should sue his body for nonsupport. His knees certainly functioned much better than they looked. I know his knees must hurt today, just like most of our body parts do because of all those hits he gave and delivered.

I began to notice during practice that none of the quarterbacks threw the ball my way, something I wasn't accustomed to when running pass patterns. On a typical practice day in Dallas, I would have caught ten or fifteen passes. But in Minnesota, neither Tommy Kramer, Steve Dils, nor the journeyman John Reaves, the former University of Florida standout, threw passes my way. I didn't see a pass for a month. I would run pass route after pass route—and nothing.

Do they think I can't catch? My nickname's Flypaper, after all. . . .

At practice one Thursday, with no passes being thrown my way, it finally dawned on me (probably later than it should have): the Vikings had picked me off waivers to keep the Cowboys from giving me a roster spot.

I walked into the huddle as Jerry Burns was about to call a play. He looked at me, looked at Sammy White, and then back at me, square in the eyes. While focused on me, Jerry called the pass play to Sammy.

His message was clear: *You're nothing, Steele! We don't need you, and we'll keep you here until we're done with you.*

I ran to the line of scrimmage, pissed off that I was being left to rot on the vine in this shithole of a practice field—a fairgrounds in the off-season, where the draught horses in the pulling competition must have felt the same mistreatment.

At home that evening, as down as I've been since waiting to find out if I had made the Cowboys roster the year before, I called Roger Staubach.

"Roger. Sorry to bother you at home. Robert Steele here. Hey, I need to know if there's anything I can do to get back with the Cowboys." He sounded happy to hear from me, though I could tell the call caught him off guard. "Roger, this place is death. I'm going to end up hating football if I don't leave here. These guys don't want me. They do not need me. They will not even throw the ball to me in practice."

Roger was always one of the nicest guys I've ever met, but even he couldn't sugarcoat a bad situation. He gave it to me straight. "Robert, your choices are pretty straightforward. You could quit, ask to be traded, or placed on waivers. The best thing you could do is stick it out and hope things get better, for what that's worth. Doesn't sound like they've done you any favors up there in Minnesota."

We made small talk for a while before I figured I had taken enough of his time.

"Thanks, Roger. I just needed to talk with someone. I'm so depressed up here. I want to play for the Cowboys, not the Vikings." The conversation was flagging because, in reality, there wasn't a damn thing I could do to save my career at that point.

The Vikings had no intention of putting me on waivers so the Cowboys could pick me up again, nor were they going to trade me. In fact, in a weird way, I understood the whole thing from a business standpoint. After all, winning games increased the team's bottom line. The gamesmanship the Vikings had been playing with my career was in the best interest of the team and its stakeholders, not me as a player or a person.

Roger tried to be positive for me, and I appreciated that. For a time, at least, with Roger's encouragement, I would change my attitude and continue to go full speed, even if the quarterbacks never threw a pass my way.

The team was at the fairgrounds the next day, and we were in sweats going through the motions for an upcoming game. Ahmad disinterestedly shuffled to the line of scrimmage play after play. Having seen enough of Ahmad's bad attitude, Coach Grant told him to pick up the pace. Ahmad continued to walk as if he hadn't heard the coach.

"Bobby, get it in gear," Coach Grant called again. (Before converting to Islam and changing his name to Ahmad Rashad, he had been Bobby Moore.)

What happened next shocked me as much as anything I've ever seen on a football field.

In an act of juvenile defiance, Ahmad held up his middle finger to Bud Grant and refused to run the route when the ball was snapped.

I was incredulous, and I looked around to see how the other guys reacted. Apparently, it was part of Ahmad's routine. Nobody else blinked an eye.

Not even Coach Grant, who just stood there shaking his head in disgust and frustration.

Ahmad was the team's unquestioned star. What could anybody do? I had just learned a small lesson about Vikings politics: Ahmad could do anything he wanted to do, and he knew it. I had to get used to it.

Reflecting on the Cowboys' politics, I would guess that Hollywood Henderson wanted to shoot a bird at Coach Landry many times. His antics off the field certainly showed a shocking level of disrespect. But even the brashest player on the Cowboys knew that there were lines you just didn't cross. The entire team would have taken him to the woodshed for that action. The Cowboys players either feared or had too much respect for Landry.

The Vikings had a very different team culture than the Cowboys. Now I knew what Bud Grant meant when he said I should fit in here. There were no rules, little discipline, and no penalties for insubordination. The inmates were running the prison.

Was this the same stoic Bud Grant I saw on television every week, the coach who had led his teams to a dozen winning seasons and had risen to the challenge so many times in one of the toughest divisions in professional football?

On Sunday, Bud Grant was all business. But during the week, anything went. Coach Landry, on the other hand, was consistent in his approach—firm every day, not just for the cameras on Sunday.

What a difference in the two organizations.

The practice facility in Dallas had everything we needed, from iced Perrier to five brands of soap, shampoo, deodorant, and shaving cream—nothing but the best for their valued players. After my first Vikings practice, I asked the equipment manager for the Vikings where the soap and shampoo were kept.

"At the grocery store," he said, looking around the locker room for a laugh from the veterans. "You bring whatever you need. Here's a towel. We do provide those."

I was in hell. I just didn't remember dying.

The gulf between Minnesota and Dallas couldn't have been more apparent than when we flew to New York in mid-October to play the Jets on Monday Night Football in the old Shea Stadium. When I was with the Cowboys, we stayed at the five-star Essex House on Central Park—first-class all the way for America's Team. We got to the field refreshed and relaxed and waxed the Jets before a national television audience.

In 1979, the trip with the Vikings was a nightmare compared to my previous experience. We stayed at a Tourway Inn on the New Jersey Turnpike, across the river from Manhattan. I didn't sleep a wink all night, fearful that one of the tractor-trailer rigs driving within a few feet of the building might veer off the highway and plow right through the middle of my room. The walls and the light fixtures shook, and every once in a while I could hear one of my teammates cursing into the dark for the noise to stop.

Of course, there was nothing for any of us to do but lie there and wait for morning.

By Monday evening, we were dog tired. We lost the game, 14–7, a foregone conclusion before we ever took the field. On the plane back to Minneapolis, we all exchanged basically the same complaint: *I didn't get any rest last night!*

I didn't say a word to my teammates about the Essex House the year before. The Vikings hated the Cowboys. The 1975 Vikings loss to the Cowboys and Drew Pearson's Hail Mary grab seemed to be coming back to haunt me, bad karma turning back onto itself. I was paying the price of seclusion for that loss, four years later. Wounds like those are slow to heal.

It didn't make things any easier, of course, that the week before the travesty in New York, the Cowboys had come to Minneapolis and waxed us, 36–20, in a game not even as close as the lopsided score would suggest.

During the run-up to the game, Bud Grant had outlined a game plan that included me. "I'm going to put a play in for you," he told me. "Players always seem to play hard against their former team the first time."

Hey, a pass play to me would be a nice change over what I've been getting.

We practiced the play, a quick screen pass with me as the target. By game time on Sunday, the grass on the infield was freshly painted green for TV—and, as always, hard as a rock.

First quarter, no quick screen pass.

Second quarter, no quick screen pass.

I figured Jerry Burns was waiting for the right time for the offense to pull off the play. I was sure of it.

Third quarter, no play called my way.

By this time, the Cowboys were ahead in the game, and no trick play was going to turn the disaster around. The game ended in a blowout.

I spoke to a few of my old teammates and told them how much I missed playing with them and trotted back to the locker room—dejected one more time.

A night on the New Jersey Turnpike was only salt in the wound.

New Competition

In mid-season, the Vikings picked up Terry LeCount, a speedster from the University of Florida. Terry became the fifth wide receiver behind Ahmad, Sammy, Doug Cunningham, and me. A five-receiver corps was a luxury few NFL teams afforded themselves. After LeCount arrived, I started to feel a little less safe in my position than I had been, and I thought maybe I was about to be cut. Oddly, the idea of leaving Minnesota didn't bother me a whole lot.

Please cut me. Put me out of my misery. Give me a chance to go to a team that might allow me to play.

Special teams were fun, but I was wasting my "flypaper hands," trying to work my way out of blocking wedges and making a tackle every once in a while—all in all, a pretty thankless job.

The sports sections of the Minneapolis newspapers started to write about the team's decision to carry five receivers.

"What are the Vikings doing with all those receivers?" asked Ralph Reeve, a veteran columnist. He was one of the harshest critics of the team's decision. Ralph approached me on one of our charter flights and tried to pump me for information.

"Robert, did you have any nicknames in college or with the Cowboys?"

"Not really." It wasn't my nature to be short with people, but I suspected the worst when Ralph initiated the conversation. He didn't even try to conceal where the conversation was going. I had learned the hard way that journalists asked questions to create an angle to hook readers. And usually, unless the storyline involved one of the star players, it didn't make the article's subject look too good.

"You must have had some kind of nickname." He threw me a wink and an elbow to get me to open up.

"Not really, Ralph. What've you heard?" I made a show of picking up a magazine and flipping through the pages.

"Come on, Robert, give me something. I want to show the people of Minneapolis some of your talents."

"OK, OK." And even as I said it, I knew my telling Ralph anything was a *huge* mistake. "Bruce Huther, my teammate with the Cowboys, called me 'Flypaper' because of my hands."

Well, Ralph's eyes lit up, and he went back to his seat. I couldn't wait to see how he might misuse our conversation for his reputation's benefit. Two days later, I opened the paper to read about my roster spot being a luxury and how the Vikings were going to cut me that week. The article wasn't a kind way to introduce me, but a more formal—and mean-spirited—dismissal. "Robert 'Flypaper' Steele is about to become 'wastepaper' this weekend," Reeve wrote. "The Vikings will not cut the well-liked Doug Cunningham, Tommy Kramer's best friend."

Even in the cutthroat world of sports journalism, when a writer would grab any crumb and try to turn it into a meal, I was stunned at what Ralph Reeve had done. That's a stab in the back I remember to this day.

Fool me once, shame on you. Fool me twice, shame on me.

I was vindicated by the fact that Reeve was wrong—way wrong. The next week, the Vikings did cut Doug Cunningham.

Oddly, my first thought wasn't relief, but panic.

Oh no! What few friends I seemed to have will turn on me. Those who didn't really accept me in the first place will hate me now.

Why did the Vikings cut Cunningham and not me? They don't want me. They don't need me. Do they think the Cowboys will pick me back up?

I found out the Cowboys had, in fact, already picked up a fourth receiver, a guy by the name of Steve Wilson who had been cut earlier in the summer at training camp.

No team carries three receivers. If I hadn't been living my own private hell in Minnesota, I would've been brought back to join the Cowboys. Clearly, the Vikings were playing games with my life and my future.

I was a pawn in a much bigger game, and I couldn't control the outcome. Instead, I just sat back and watched—almost as if none of this had anything to do with me—the moves the Vikings made on their giant chessboard.

What was worse was what happened later that same week Cunningham was cut. Tensions were beginning to show as the season wore on. Players were beginning to snap at each other. For me, I kept my distance until someone pushed the wrong button. We were lining up in the huddle and Dave Huffman, a well-liked rookie center and the team's second-round draft pick out of Notre Dame, said something smart to me as I lined up directly across from him in the huddle. I told him to back off. Before I could even react, he kicked me as hard as he could between my legs, a direct hit on my male anatomy. I hit the ground.

I couldn't practice for three days. Huffman wasn't fined or disciplined, and I took the rest of the week to heal. He never apologized, and no one on the team ever said anything to me about the incident. This collection of players was no team. They had no stadium of their own, no practice facility, no discipline, and no character. What we did have was Tommy Kramer leading the team to the local watering hole after every practice. The season's outcome spoke volumes.

This was Bud Grant's *Animal House.*

Again, I realized that my stay there wasn't welcome, and someone had forgotten to tell Bud Grant or Jerry Burns to cut me instead of Doug Cunningham. I didn't play that weekend but was able to come back the week after that. I never forgot that experience—no male ever does. My groin turned black, blue, and purple and swelled to the size of two baseballs. I've never even seen pictures that looked as bad as that. Yet the only thing the trainers said to me was "that looks terrible" and "that is the worst case I have ever seen." Words weren't going to heal that wound, and staying with the Vikings just made it that much worse.

An incident toward the end of the season made me wonder if things could get any worse.

We were getting ready to play the Detroit Lions on the Sunday after Thanksgiving. Our Saturday walk-through practice, which normally started at 10:00 a.m., was delayed about fifteen minutes because Tommy Kramer hadn't shown up. He finally did make it, obviously worse for wear from the night before, ten minutes before practice ended. I thought it would have been the perfect time for Bud Grant to step in and discipline Kramer.

When kickoff time came on Sunday, I fully expected Steve Dils, a talented quarterback out of Stanford, to take the field as the starter. But there was Tommy Kramer headed out to take the snaps instead. Bud believed a hungover quarterback was his better choice. For sure, Kramer was himself a talented player, even if he didn't always prepare as well as he should have. And that day, we managed to squeak by the hapless Detroit Lions, 14–7 (the Lions were 1–10 at the time, and the effort must have fired up the team—they won their next game and finished the season 2–14).

More Drug Queries

One of the Vikings' defensive linemen, and one of the stalwarts on a unit that some fans still call the "Purple People Eaters" for their ferocity, came up to me and pantomimed popping pills, putting an invisible handful in his mouth and swallowing.

I'm sure I looked confused. At the time, I had no idea what he was doing.

The next time I saw him, after a meeting break, he did it again.

And then a third and a fourth time.

By then, I'd had enough. I finally stopped him and said, "What in the hell are you doing?"

I couldn't believe his response.

"The word out of Dallas is you've got a line on something special, something you never shared with anybody."

"What the hell do you mean, something special?"

"You know, some kind of upper. Poppers, shit like that. Come on, Steele, let me in on your little secret."

"Why would anybody think I was on uppers?"

"Man, because you run around here like the Tasmanian Devil all the time. Full speed, everywhere. You're on something, and we all want some of it. It must be good stuff." He leaned in close. "Come on, Steele. For the team."

I shook my head and pushed him away from me.

"Stop it!" I shouted. "You think I am on drugs because I run full speed every play? How pathetic is that? The only way I could actually go full speed is with drugs? What about just going out and playing hard?" This big lineman, someone I had thought was a top-notch football player, just stood there with his big arms crossed and a grin on his face. "Who told you I was on poppers? Who was it?"

He shook his head, like he was disappointed that I wouldn't let him in on the secret.

"That's cool, Steele. If you're not on anything, just forget about it. But if you are, you know, maybe think about sharing it. For the team."

"I'm not on anything. Quit being a jerk."

He walked away, mumbling more to himself than to me, "That's cool. No harm in asking, you know. . . ."

So much for the romantic and glorious world of gladiatorial combat in the National Football League.

If coaches and team owners don't value team members any more than they showed me by keeping me on the shelf so that I couldn't play in Dallas, how the hell could the players be expected to value themselves?

The next weekend confirmed my desire to leave the Vikings.

We were 4–5 and about to play the Saint Louis Cardinals in Busch Stadium, a place where I had some good memories from the previous season. It was there I had hit their wide receiver on a kickoff, and he jumped up and congratulated me—kind of a welcome-to-the-NFL moment between two young guys living a shared dream.

In early November, as a member of the Vikings, I went into the visitors' locker room thinking, like I did every weekend, that this would be the week I'd get a chance to play. Walking over to the urinals, I noticed an unusual buzz going around the locker room. I asked one of the players what was going on.

"Nothing," he insisted. He was agitated and wouldn't look me in the eye.

A few minutes later, we headed out for the opening kickoff. We were favored to win the game, and maybe just a little eager to prove our worth. A win in Saint Louis would be the difference between getting back to .500 and scuttling our chances at making the play-offs.

Even when we should have been focused on the game, though, the buzz continued.

"What's going on with you guys?" I asked another player.

"Somebody left the stuff at home," he said, shaking his head in disappointment. "Doc won't give us any."

My mouth dropped. I realized then why I was so different and didn't fit in, as Bud Grant had suggested I would. The "stuff" was uppers, and a handful of players were so insecure in their ability to get the job done on the field that they couldn't convince themselves to play the game without the drugs.

That was unbelievable to me on a professional football team. Not only did we not play our best that day, we were blown out of Busch Stadium, humiliated 37–7 and all but knocked out of the play-off hunt.

One thing—one good thing—happened in the game that made my career. I was thrown my only pass in a regular season game. I made the catch, which put me in the NFL record books.

One pass thrown my way, one catch made.

"Flypaper" might not become "wastepaper" after all.

In an otherwise disappointing season, the other highlight was in Buccaneer Stadium in Tampa Bay. Ricky Bell was having an unbelievable season, and the Bucs were climbing out of the cellar of the "Black and Blue" Central division of the NFC. Tampa always had trouble hanging with Chicago, Green Bay, and Minnesota, so a bright light like Ricky Bell was welcome relief for Bucs' fans from the usual double-digit loss seasons they had posted in their first three years in the league (infamously, the Bucs lost their first twenty-six games in the league).

That week, the game was typical NFC Central football, two good defenses going head to head. The lead changed hands several times in a close game, and going into the third quarter we were down by four points. We got a stop on defense and, as Tampa set up in punt formation, I lined up over center.

Coach Steckel put on a block, knowing we had to make something happen. I got a good jump on the snap and slid past the center, remembering the moves that helped me make the Cowboys when Ditka just about lost his mind in anger at his players' inability to block me. Untouched, I blocked the punt. One of our defensive backs picked up the ball and ran for a touchdown.

We won the game, and I was awarded a game ball for the effort. I had now accomplished my second football goal.

The Vikings finished the 1979 season with a whimper, losing two of the last three and staying home from the play-offs with a lackluster 7–9 record.

Flying back to Dallas to pick up my Trans Am and drive back to Columbus seemed like a welcome relief. The bright spot was that on this December day, it was a balmy forty-nine degrees with the sun shining and certainly not Minnesota winter weather.

The off-season was difficult. In September, my father suffered his first heart attack just after Hurricane Frederic had wiped out the two apartment projects he owned in Mobile, Alabama, and Pascagoula, Mississippi. Since I was available after the football season, I offered to move to Mobile to oversee a $3 million restoration of both complexes. I could work out every day, stay in shape, and keep my father's company intact. It was the least I could do for my family. Dad agreed, and I drove to Mobile in my Trans Am, my steady companion through a lot of good and tough times in my two years in the league.

I learned a lot of valuable lessons in Mobile that spring. First, many people will take advantage of you. Second, helping out your family is always the right thing to do, even when you know you should have been doing something different. I should have been in Minneapolis, just like I had been in Dallas, getting ready for the next season and bonding with my teammates. Finally, I learned that when money is involved people will do strange things. That family secret will have to remain just that—a secret.

Despite everything that had happened in the off-season, I reported to training camp that summer in great shape. My 1.9 percent body fat was intact, and I could still run all day without getting tired. Even though the Vikings never ran wind sprints, a far cry from the rigorous training I endured with the Cowboys, I always wanted them to. Of course, that the Vikings didn't have any real practice facilities also meant very few players stayed in Minneapolis for the cold winter and spring. Most bugged out of town as soon as the season ended, except the Minnesota diehards. I didn't spend time with any of the players. My usual off-season daily grind of running pass patterns and perfecting my timing with the quarterbacks didn't happen, and I felt like I was still a new kid coming in for my third NFL season, my second with the Vikings.

Something as simple as not bonding with teammates is so often the difference between champions and also-rans, and every time I thought about the Minnesota Vikings, I realized that the team would continue to wallow in relative obscurity until some major changes were made in the way the team was run.

One More Year?

In July 1980, I arrived on the Minnesota State University campus at Mankato, home of the Minnesota Vikings training camp. In the off-season, despite some serious misgivings as to my role on the team and my future in the league, I devoted myself to becoming a bona fide member of the Vikings.

I'll put up with their nonsense and, eventually, they'll begin to throw to me. One of the receivers might get hurt, and I have to be ready to play. I won't give up or give in.

I was having a typical summer camp, catching the few balls the quarterbacks threw my way. In our first couple of preseason games, I played special teams, as usual, and started to settle in to the system and the rhythms of another season.

After that game, though, I was hit with a phone call that changed my life. My mother was crying on the other end of the line. "Your grandmother Gladys has just died, Robert. The funeral will be Thursday. We need you here."

A thousand memories of my dear grandmother flashed through my mind. I went numb. "Of course, Mom. I'll be on the next plane."

The team was in mid-week preparations for our final pre-season game against the Miami Dolphins at the Orange Bowl, where we had played that epic Super Bowl against the Pittsburgh Steelers. I was looking forward to playing again in Miami and seeing the Dolphin cheerleader I met the previous year. I certainly wasn't looking forward to the funeral. Grandma Gladys was the first familiar, loving person in my family to die, and she had been a significant part of my life. I wanted to support my family and honor Gladys's memory.

I found Les Steckel and told him I had to go to Atlanta for a funeral. I would, I said, meet the team in Miami on Friday. He frowned, gave me a troubled, pensive look, and shrugged his shoulders.

Hey, I'm not asking to go to Disneyland or play hooky. I'm going to the funeral of a family member.

The Funeral

Grandmother Gladys's funeral was an emotional experience, and I cried as much during her funeral as I had in my entire life. I couldn't get myself together. Gladys was one of the funniest, craziest people I've ever known. She never met a stranger, and a lot of folks always said that my personality came from her. We were similar people, loved life, and saw the positive side of things, even in the down times. Her absence depressed me terribly.

I wanted to spend more time in Atlanta after the funeral, but I had an obligation to the team (misguided, perhaps, considering the way the team obviously felt about me). I boarded a plane to Miami at my own expense and met the team for that Sunday's game. I played the next day, tears flowing. I never let any of the players or coaches see me cry. I didn't think they would understand.

I moved through the game on autopilot. Charging down the field on kick coverage was like trying to walk on the bottom of a pool. I wasn't aware of winning or losing the game, only the loss that I felt at Gladys's death. The team had put in an audible that week while I was away. The audible was very clear. If the quarterback saw a blitz coming, the receiver to the blitz side would do a quick slant. I was playing in the second half when I began a route and the ball flew past my right ear, landing on the ground behind me. I stayed on the field for punt team, and when I ran off after the tackle I was met by Steckel telling me I blew the blitz call. Not sure what had just happened, I told him I was sorry. It was a simple audible, but I missed it because I wasn't in Minnesota for that practice and nobody told me about it until after the game. So I got blamed for missing an audible I didn't know anything about. It was strange, almost surreal in hindsight, to think that I walked off the Orange Bowl turf not realizing I had just played the last football game of my life.

I got another shock when we returned to Minneapolis, but this time I couldn't have been happier. On Monday morning, the coaching staff released me from the Vikings.

Cut, finished, eliminated from the team in the final cut.

Gladys, I've had another death this week, but I'm celebrating!

Instead of being sad or angry, I felt a relief I'd never felt before, a freedom missing from my time with the Vikings.

And now, I thought, I had a newfound opportunity to catch on with another team.

Heading Home

I packed my car and headed south, knowing in my gut this was the break I wanted. In the NFL, the final cut is the worst time for a player to be let go. All the teams have just solidified their rosters for the season, and any team picking up a free agent after their forty-five-man roster is in place has to change the plans it has already made.

Despite what you hear about how innovative and agile a league the NFL is when it comes to finding new ways to win games, coaches and front offices are never keen to change horses in mid-stream without an injury or something significant to its corps of receivers.

So for the next six weeks, no calls. Not even a nibble. All I could do was sit and wait—something I was not good at then and am not good at today.

Didn't I have the best hands on the Cowboys? Why isn't the phone ringing? Should I get an agent and see if that helps? Should I think about putting football behind me?

More questions without answers—the story of my life.

Red Zone Rules

R-E-S-P-E-C-T

"I feared and respected Coach Landry. I respected him because of who he was and what he represented. I feared him because he was tough and fair," says Drew Pearson. "He was very tough, and you wanted to please him. When he walked by, you straightened up. When Landry walked in the room, the room got quiet.

"That's respect, and he had earned every bit of it with his actions over the years."

Become a Go-To Guy

"Robert was, first of all, an outstanding individual. He was one of those guys you never had to worry about. He did what he was supposed to, when he was supposed to. What I remember most about him was in calling plays during the course of the game, I could always count on Robert," says Bill Baker, former coach at North Alabama.

"If we needed a first down, we knew we could go to Robert. He was a big, tall kid—one of the bigger receivers in the conference at the time—and we could rely on him when we really needed to get that big first down, make that big play or score a touchdown. He always responded very well."

Accept, Adapt, Achieve

Changes can be painfully difficult to adjust to. My move to the Vikings was tougher than I'd even imagined. My loyalty was divided, and I happened not to be where I wanted to be.

You may well find yourself in a similar situation at some point in life. All I can say is, "Hang on, it will get better, and try to enjoy the ride."

When you're at the depth of despair, simply trust that one day, somehow, things will get better.

When you start over, you have to learn a whole new system. I've never been afraid of learning new things in football or any other field. Whatever your field, don't be afraid to learn something new. It'll help you improve and grow in countless ways.

Being with the Cowboys and then with the Vikings was a lesson for me on excellence. I was able to compare and contrast, and there was no comparison! But the experience wasn't entirely in vain. It reinforced within me what was of value and what true excellence means.

Another thing I learned, in hindsight, is that you can't always control your circumstances or your environment. What you can control is your *attitude*. Maybe my early attitude with the Vikings wasn't the best. Maybe I could have done more to ingratiate myself to the team, to make myself valuable. Had I succeeded in improving my attitude, perhaps the experience would have been more bearable.

And finally, wherever you are, whatever you're doing, even if you're in a situation you find far from ideal, you can still accomplish your goals. When I was feeling most miserable, I was still able to accomplish my second football goal.

I'm immensely proud of that.

17

A Letter to Landry

The First Day of the Rest of My Life. . . .

The day I got cut by the Minnesota Vikings was the first day of the rest of my life.

After a drought where teams seemed to be avoiding me like a four-game losing streak, two teams—the San Francisco 49ers and the Tampa Bay Buccaneers—showed an interest in me. I ran four forty-yard dashes for both, and my speed was still intact. I was running great pass patterns and caught the ball well.

An interesting conversation in the locker room of the 49ers was with one of their assistants. He came by and told me how well I had performed and that they would "be in touch." He then turned and said, "I understand you are working on your master's degree." I told him I had not started but wanted to while I was playing. He grinned and walked away. I never figured out what he meant by that comment, but I never heard back from them. Nor did I attain my master's degree.

And neither team offered me a contract.

I was so naïve to the entire league's political process that I never bothered to hire an agent (unthinkable today, even for free agents who have little chance of making a team) who would have gotten me in front of teams needing a veteran receiver with some skill.

Hindsight, right?

I went to work in the insurance business, thinking I would pass the time until the call came. After working as hard I had to get a foot in the door in the NFL, I never considered for an instant that my career was over, only temporarily on hold.

And then things began to change.

A funny incident showed me how people really think about professional athletes. One day I was getting ready for a business meeting, sitting at a diner and reading my materials, when a man leaned over said, "Robert, what's it like going from a business like professional football, where everybody wants to talk to you, to a business like insurance, where *nobody* wants to talk to you?"

It was the first time I had ever heard that question!

I thought about it for a second, smiled politely, and said, "Actually, the two are similar. Both are in the public eye. Both provide a valuable service. And in both, success is dependent on the person being a motivated self-starter. I like them both."

The humor was not lost. They had their laugh, and I went and closed a deal. Sweet revenge.

Crossroads

The newspapers reported that Dan Reeves had just left the Dallas Cowboys to become the head coach for the Denver Broncos, the team the Cowboys beat in the 1978 Super Bowl XII. I felt real joy for Dan. He certainly deserved the promotion, and he would be a mainstay in the NFL for twenty-three seasons, coaching

Denver, the New York Giants, and Atlanta to 190 wins and 4 Super Bowl appearances.

Three weeks after taking the helm, Coach Reeves called and asked me if I would be interested in signing on with the Broncos as a free agent.

As good as the offer sounded—and I was flattered he would even think of me after becoming head coach—I hesitated. On one hand, here was my shot to get back in the game with a team that would value my skills. I knew Coach Reeves would give me a fair shot.

On the other hand, as soon as the book had seemingly closed on my football career, I had immediately set some goals for myself in the insurance business. I wanted to get my designation as a Chartered Life Underwriter (CLU), the highest level in the insurance profession. I wanted to make the Million Dollar Round Table. I wanted to qualify for the company's annual sales convention.

And I would need to continue selling to accomplish those goals.

To make the Broncos' roster, I needed to get back in shape, fly to Denver on my own nickel, and become acclimated to the altitude (no small thing, if you've ever done any strenuous physical activity more than five thousand feet above sea level), the players, and an offense with some new wrinkles in it.

Still, I figured a chance like this would never come again.

I decided to take a shot at resurrecting my football career, but only after I took the first two exams for the CLU designation before leaving for Denver. I would pay my way for this early acclimation period by staying in a local hotel until training camp opened. I could put the time to good use working out and getting in top shape. Coach Reeves and I discussed my time in Dallas, agreeing that my experiences there would be invaluable as I worked out in Denver. There was only one difference in

Denver—I didn't get an apartment this time, and everything I spent was coming out of my own pocket.

So much for perks.

Still, I was looking forward to training camp, and I trained for four weeks as hard as I had in Dallas three seasons before. The day before training camp opened, I pulled a hamstring running my usual ten 110-yard sprints. As soon as I pulled up lame, I knew that my first hamstring injury of any kind would make my time with the Broncos a short-lived experience. Spending time as a brand-new player, not having signed any waivers this time, would limit me more than I knew. "You can't make the club in the tub," the old saying goes. I tried everything I knew to heal and strengthen my leg, but I wasn't able to run full speed when the time came.

The first week of camp was frustrating. I was in great shape, but the hamstring tweak didn't allow me to stand out. I suited up on Saturday and tried to run a pass pattern in my first drill and just could not push off as I did in all of my other camps. I called home to tell them I was done and would be going to see Coach Reeves the next morning. Dad said he had an envelope, and from The American College with my name on it. I told him this was my grades for the first two exams. He opened the envelope, and sure enough I had passed the first two CLU exams. At that moment, things started to come into focus for me. Those grades put me well on my way toward my goal of becoming a CLU.

Maybe my leg was telling me it wasn't willing to run full speed for the Broncos. I had already chosen another road, zoomed full speed ahead in a new direction. Deep inside, I didn't want to go back to the NFL, and I finally realized I couldn't recreate my golden year with the Dallas Cowboys.

That night, I made up my mind. My football career was over.

I went to see Dan Reeves the next morning to tell him I was done. He knew my heart wasn't in it—he could see the obvious difference in my intensity level after watching me bust my ass to make the team in Dallas—and we parted on the best of terms. I wished him well in Denver, and Coach Reeves went on to honor the game with his integrity and his innovation.

Football was a memory for me.

My business career was taking off, and I was moving forward. I would never look back with any regrets on my brief professional football career.

When the decision was made, I was at peace with myself and felt a freedom I hadn't felt in a long time.

Retrospective

As I look back on my football career and transition into the business world, I realize I had accomplished more than I probably should have.

Being an underdog for most of my life meant having to work harder and smarter, staying mentally focused, and always adjusting to life's challenges. My Little League football coaches, Buford Parker and Frank Allen, taught me the fundamentals. I continued to learn how to better apply those techniques through junior high, high school, and college.

Many coaches helped me in that journey, like Wallace Davis from Hardaway High in Columbus. He loved his players, and he still does. Bill Baker at the University of North Alabama believed in my ability and told the scout Walt Yaworski that I was his rising star on that glorious spring afternoon before college graduation. Jim Goodman, my position coach at UNA and the older brother to my college quarterback, Gerald Goodman, taught me the "tricks of the trade."

I became a sure-handed receiver because of the fundamentals Coach Goodman taught me. He played as big a part of my overall football success as any other coach, standing over me while I did fingertip pushups until my hands could catch footballs one-handed from thirty yards away.

The biggest lesson I learned from football wasn't sports-related, but focused on the importance of setting goals, achieving them—and then always setting new ones, without resting on any laurels.

I set two goals for myself when I signed with the Cowboys. The first was to make the team, which I did. The second was to get a game ball, which I received from the Vikings instead of the Cowboys.

The most valuable lesson of all: Set a goal and accomplish it, and set another goal and accomplish that one as well. Then, make sure you set another goal. You can never stop setting goals for yourself.

I realized a few years later that I accomplished the two goals I set for myself in professional football. But I did not set another goal to accomplish. When I did not have another goal to reach, football was out of my life.

Letter to Coach Landry

Coach Tom Landry's influence on me was significant, and I was prepared to tell him as much when he came to Columbus, Georgia, in 1991 to speak to the Fellowship of Christian Athletes and play in their sponsored golf tournament. Since I had played for Coach Landry, I also participated in the event and arranged our flights with a good friend of mine, fellow pilot Jack Pezold, to Columbus, Augusta, and Dalton over the course of two days.

Other than a once-in-a-lifetime chance to play golf at Augusta National, Coach Landry's visit would be an opportunity to spend quality time with a man I genuinely admired.

It was a special time, not only because I enjoyed Coach's company, but because he met my parents, who died in 2002.

Listening to Coach speak of his faith, family, and football was as much a gift to me as it was for anybody in the standing-room-only audiences. Coach Landry could have told tales of athletes like Hollywood Henderson that would have made parents' hair stand on end. But he chose to share the positives of football—the game and the profession—weaving his experiences with the confidence of a skilled storyteller into life lessons no one could ever forget. Audiences clamored for more.

Our day at Augusta National was like a dream. Riding down Magnolia Lane, the tree-lined drive that leads to the famous clubhouse, I felt honored by the rare opportunity so few golfers experience in their lives. As awestruck as I was by the golf course, I was more in awe of Coach Landry, whom I hadn't seen in more than a decade. I soaked up the moment.

Coach Landry played well, birdying the first hole (I three-putted), and mixing in pars and bogeys the rest of the way. Coming through Amen corner—holes 11, 12, and 13 and often the deciding stretch of golf in the Masters every April—my day was coming to a close. I had a deep desire to thank Coach for the opportunities he gave me.

I could see he loved playing golf. He was relaxed yet competitive as we toured the hallowed grounds of Augusta National. Golf is the ultimate sport because you only compete with yourself, work to improve based on your own goals—and always know, no matter how well you play, that you can do better. Sitting in the fairway on number 13, the tough hole that has the infamous creek protecting the approach shot, the caddy told me to hit a seven iron in front of the creek to lay up and play it safe. As I was taking my swing, I stopped at the top and looked at the caddy. "Give me my three wood; there ain't no lay up in my game." I hit it well, and the ball flew the creek and landed in one of the bunkers guarding the green. I couldn't go to number fourteen without taking a shot at the green in two.

I managed a birdie on the par-five fifteenth, hitting the green in two and putting two. Walking up the eighteenth hole with Coach Landry felt like we were walking up the last fairway of our lives, a moment to be remembered. We shook hands after completing our round, and I told Coach how much I had enjoyed his company.

When the scores were tallied, Coach Landry had bested me by a single shot.

One shot. One shot.

That one shot I had of making the Cowboys so long ago settled in my mind as we boarded the private plane headed for Dalton to another speech and another round of golf at the Farm, a course owned by the carpet king, Bob Shaw.

But my experience at Augusta kept rattling around in my mind.

One shot.

The one shot continued to haunt me as I looked for an opportunity to thank Coach Landry for what I had come to think of as my Golden Year, the 1978 season with the Dallas Cowboys. I wanted to share what he had done for me, what he had meant to so many players, and the positive impact he had on his players, the fans, and the entire sports world.

Could I get the courage to thank him? What exactly would I say? Would he understand the impact he and the rest of the Cowboys organization had had on my life even though I only played one season for him?

I never put the words together or had the opportunity to be alone with him for even a moment. People wanted his time and his attention, always wanting a piece of him. As usual, he was gracious enough to share himself on that trip, as he had on so many other occasions over the years.

As much as I wanted to express my gratitude to Coach Landry, I never had another chance to spend time with him.

On February 12, 2000, Tom Landry died.

The Cowboys organization and the world mourned the loss of a great man. Although Tex Schram was the marketing genius who coined the Cowboys' famous nickname, Coach Landry had built the team, setting lofty goals, taking individuals from all walks of life and backgrounds, and molding them into a team—America's Team.

That's just a little of what I wish I could have mustered the courage to share with him before he died.

Instead, I wrote this letter, hoping someday to share my thoughts with anyone who would be interested in knowing a little bit more about this great man.

Dear Coach Landry,

Didn't we have a wonderful round of golf, strolling the famous fairways of Augusta National, as so many golf legends have? Playing that course was like playing in Texas Stadium—two legendary places that have witnessed countless battles by fierce competitors.

So many emotions went through my mind on the golf course, and I wanted to take an opportunity to share with you the impact you've made on my life—and the lives of everyone I've ever touched.

The opportunity you and the rest of the organization gave me in 1978 was my golden moment. Signing that free agent contract and knowing I would be suiting up with the World Champion Cowboys was a dream come true. The fact that I was an underdog trying to make the team had a profound impact on my life, something I would fully appreciate only much later.

The lessons I learned from watching you and the Cowboys organization taught me business and personal skills that I should have been awarded an MBA for—

one season of experience with the Cowboys, a lifetime of lessons.

I'm sure you understand the positive influence you've had on hundreds of ballplayers through the years and the thousands of others who dreamed to play for the Cowboys and never made the team. Even the fans, the media, the front office staff, and your coaches were influenced by the way you lived your life—with unwavering integrity.

You and I only had brief moments together. But in those moments, I felt like I was taking a part of you with me, from the first time I met you to our last football conversation as I headed to the Minnesota Vikings, and then a decade later on the FCA whirlwind tour around Georgia. I was thankful you had the time and opportunity to meet my parents, who also admired you a great deal and spoke of you often even long after my football career was over.

I know I sound like an ordinary fan, and I suppose I am. While I became a part of the team, I remained loyal to the organization even while playing for the Vikings. I wore purple and gold, but I bled blue and silver. The Cowboys organization changed my life and the lives of millions of people. The true impact of your life on others continues to be felt.

I wish I had been able to say these words in person the last time I saw you. Maybe this letter isn't a missed opportunity, but one more opportunity—to change lives and to encourage dreams.

Sincerely,

Robert Steele
Dallas Cowboys 1978

Lessons from Football and Beyond

Several years later, I was asked to write a series of articles about the insurance business from a sales and marketing perspective. The first article I wrote was titled "What Landry, Reeves, and Ditka Taught Me about . . . Business." The piece focused on what I learned from these three giants.

Coach Landry, the ultimate CEO, had a philosophy of coaching the coaches, which allowed the coaches to coach the players—a business model that still works today. Landry often seemed aloof to players, and he didn't allow himself to get close to any player. Although I didn't know Coach well—who did?—I believe that the wall of separation wasn't what Landry the man would have chosen. Rather, the wall protected him from the public and fans so he could accomplish his goals.

Reeves taught me to be a student of the game—to know your opponent, to know your game plan, to execute successfully—no matter which game it was.

Ditka taught me about passion, the fierce intensity needed to run through a brick wall or a blocker. Ditka was a student of the game himself, but what separated him from every other coach I've ever known was his maniacal, single-minded passion. It served him well.

Goals and the passion to see them through have pushed me in my business career more than anything else. The idea of setting goals, accomplishing goals, adjusting to changing conditions, learning people, and being always aware of what is going on around me—all those skills have helped me accomplish my goals from the moment I put away cleats for the last time until today, more than thirty years later.

Since joining the Cowboys, I've never been the same. I'm confident that every teammate and every player who donned a Cowboy uniform in a preseason practice or a game—and certainly those on the regular season roster for any of the Landry years—feels the same way.

We were part of a legend that lives on. We were part of America's Team.

Epilogue

Life After Football— Thirty Years Later

I remember my grandfather and my father telling me stories when I was young about things they did and how they said that it felt like yesterday when they were reliving these stories.

Guess what? All these years later, I feel the same way.

I look back and can't imagine it's been thirty years since I put on my last helmet. Thirty years gone in a flash.

I got married, had four children, started three companies, got elected—and defeated—in the political process. I've seen good times and hard times personally, professionally, and financially.

What have I learned along the way?

I guess you could say I've learned a lot—and very little. I've discovered quite a bit about people, for one thing. Being involved in sales and marketing, you get to know people—sometimes more than you'd like to know. Both the buyers and non-buyers teach you a lot about yourself and how to adapt or adjust your product and your style along the way.

People are amazing creatures. They live, laugh, love, learn, lead, and leave. Each of these words means different things to different people because of every person's unique world view. But in the end, those are the words most apt to describe people's thoughts, actions, words, and deeds.

I'm often asked about how much sports I watch on TV. You might find this odd, but I hardly ever watch a complete game on the tube. In fact, for almost twenty of the years since I've hung up the spikes for the last time, I wouldn't watch a whole game. Sure, I might catch a play or two or a portion of a play-off game, or maybe tune in to the Super Bowl to watch the commercials. I enjoyed playing sports, though, so I got involved in golf right after football because I was told it was a good "business" game. I found that to be true. (It took me much longer to learn that no business is actually conducted on the course; rather, it's the relationships developed on the course that carry over to the office or the boardroom.)

The biggest adjustment for me is dealing with the aches and pains, remnants from too many practices, too many games, too much wear and tear on a body not truly equipped to have been there in the first place. Pick a joint, any joint, and I'll tell you it hurts. Not bad enough to do anything about it, but enough to remind me when and where I injured it in the first place.

Would I go through it all again, knowing what I know now? Absolutely!

Would I do things differently? You bet.

But I would still play football for the Dallas Cowboys a thousand times over as the lowest-paid player on the team, and I would never look back. These days, I pay almost as much a year for my chiropractor and massage therapy as I made playing the game. But the game—the Cowboys, the coaches, the players, and the experience—taught me lessons I wouldn't have learned anywhere else. Lessons I *couldn't* have learned anywhere else.

What would I have done differently? I would've focused more on football, earlier on, and dedicated much more time to developing my body physically. And I would have become a much more intense student of the game. I missed out on a lot of things because of these sins of omission. I was blessed with great hands to catch the football, great hand-eye coordination, and a great ability to take physical punishment. I wasn't blessed with blinding speed, but I could've made myself better, bigger, and even faster through more disciplined physical preparation.

Could I have played longer? I think so, but who ever knows? With extra conditioning, more attention to the details, maybe I could have squeezed out a couple more seasons. Those extra seasons of busting up wedges would have paid a price that I might not have wanted to pay. So, I look back thankful for my two seasons and thankful that was all I got.

I feel blessed to have gotten the opportunities I had. In a strange way, if I had actually done all the things I mention above, I might have made it to the NFL under much different circumstances and wouldn't have gotten a chance to make the Cowboys as a free agent in 1978.

So, no regrets. I'm a blessed man, blessed with experiences and knowledge and relationships that have made me a more complete person as a result of my sports background.

Sports prepared me for my life as a salesman. My experience showed me income potential. If I wanted to have the nicer things in life, then I needed income. Sales offered the opportunity to have more than just a nine-to-five job. That work also showed me that the harder I applied myself, the more I was able to make. The more experience I gained, the easier it would become to generate more and more income. I finally broke the $100,000, $250,000, $500,000 and $750,000 barriers of annual income. Pretty good considering the paltry salary my first year in the NFL.

I still have goals. I still feel like I am "green and growing," because I know when I stop learning and taking on new experiences—when I stop *doing*—then I've become ripe and it's only a matter of time before the rot sets in. No one wants to rot, a lesson I learned from my father, who never wanted to retire and never truly did.

Let me leave you with five tips, whether you're 12, 22, 42, 62, or even 82:

1. It ain't over until the game, the season, the business deal, your time with family, and even your life has ended. There are always lessons to be learned, experiences to savor, memories to share, and successes beyond your wildest imagination. Dream *big* dreams. Don't live your life only to look back with regret and say, "I wish I had only dreamt bigger." Do it now. Don't wait. The life you lose will be your own. *Carpe diem.* Seize the day—and seize your life.

2. Play every play as if it were your last. Every play means every play, whether it be a play in a game or a play in a meeting, event, business deal, or with your family and friends. Give your best effort every day, every play. I beat myself up constantly over this, because I sometimes think in business I have time to rest or relax. But others are relying on you. That's why you are part of a team. Contribute more than your fair share. Pull more than your load. Make your presence more than just known—make an impact. Make it now!

3. One day you'll look back and want to write your own story. Do it. Start making notes. Keep a journal. Write down life's everyday oddities. Record little events that ended up changing the outcome of a game, event, or business deal before you forget about those details and have to rely on memory. Your memory of big events in your life will always be good. What you'll forget—and these details are important—are the little things that

actually mattered in the ultimate outcome of your life. Little things, combined together, often are the impetus for much bigger accomplishments. Being the underdog my entire life has taught me to value the little things, because I had to work harder than all of my counterparts and had to watch jealously as other people seemed to come by things naturally. Now that I look back and see what really happened, though, it's like I was playing a part in a movie and watching the script unfold. And I'm glad that I paid attention to the details, so I could write my story for anybody who wanted to hear it.

4. Don't be afraid to reinvent yourself. I have had to do this several times along the journey. Take every obstacle, closed door, lost job, failed relationship, failed class, failed project, or failed initiative as an opportunity to begin again more intelligently this time around. Reinventing yourself means taking stock of who you are, what strengths you have, and what you truly love to do, and finding a way to do that. As the old saying goes, if you love what you do, then what you do is no longer work. It is a joy and not a job. I hate jobs. But I love to invest myself in things I enjoy. There goes that "joy" word again. Invest in yourself. Invest in the people you love. Invest in the things that will matter ten years from now, not ten minutes from now.

5. Know and understand there are rules to live by. I mentioned them earlier in what I call my Red Zone Rules. I try to keep my Red Zone Rules close to me and always a part of everything I do. As I have said before, the red zone is where it's at. It is where the offense is in a position to score. Everyone loves to score.

What a wonderful journey life has been. There were good times, there were difficult times. But there truly were never any bad times. "Life is good," the old truism goes. Amen to that. Life *is* truly good. If you're reading this and are over fifty, you're thankful for so many things and regret a few. We all do. If you are between the ages of thirty and fifty, you'll realize soon enough just how fast those years flew by. You won't believe it today, no matter what I tell you. But it's true.

Time flies.

Hold on for the wild ride.

Invest in yourself, invest in your family, and invest in the future. All are great investments. All will pay dividends.

About the Author

Robert Steele is a former wide receiver for the Dallas Cowboys and a participant in Super Bowl XIII. Robert is CEO of TheEnterpriseZone, providing sales, marketing, and business development consulting in the healthcare, insurance, employee benefits, and financial services markets. Robert is currently working on his second book about his days with the Cowboys. He has also served in the Georgia State Legislature as an elected state representative is a private pilot and an avid golfer. Robert enjoys speaking to youth groups, sales groups, and executives on a variety of business, sales, and motivational topics.

Photos

Steele family photo ca. 1960–1961

From a feature story in the Dallas Cowboys Weekly, 1978.
The author standing beside his 1978 Pontiac Trans Am—similar to
the car driven by Burt Reynolds in *Smokey and the Bandit.*

The author's first return to watch a UNA game, 1978. Athletic Trainer Johnny Long is
talking to him about the Cowboys and all of the knee surgeries he endured.

Cowboys vs. Cardinals, Busch Stadium, 1978

The author in practice with the Dallas Cowboys, 1978.

The author in practice with the Dallas Cowboys.
No. 32 Dennis Thurmond provides coverage, 1978.

The author in practice with the Dallas Cowboys, 1978.

Dallas Cowboys autograph picture, 1978.

The NFC Championship ring, made by Jostens for the
1978 NFC Champion Dallas Cowboys.

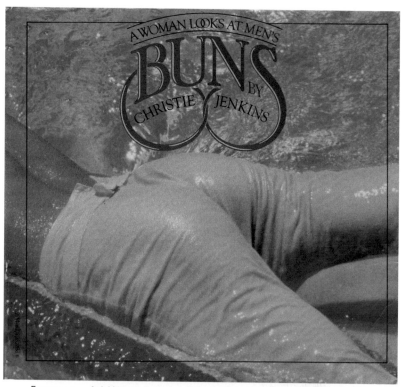

Front cover of *A Woman's Look at Men's Buns* by Christie Jenkins (1980).

ROBERT STEELE

The author's picture in *A Woman's Look at Men's Buns* by
Christie Jenkins (1980). Dallas Cowboys training camp, Cal
Lutheran College, Thousand Oaks, California, 1979.

THE DALLAS COWBOYS

Other Dallas Cowboys included in *A Woman's Look at Men's Buns*
by Christie Jenkins (1980).

The author at a speech to eMoney Advisors, Napa Valley, California, 2009.